SECRETS OF HAPPY RELATIONSHIPS

50 Techniques to Stay in Love

Jenny Hare

D0106670

SECRETS OF HAPPY RELATIONSHIPS

50 Techniques to Stay in Love

Jenny Hare

First published in Great Britain in 2014 by Hodder & Stoughton. An Hachette UK company.

First published in US in 2014 by The McGraw-Hill Companies, Inc.

This edition published 2014

British Library Cataloguing in Publication Data: a catalogue record for this title is available from the British Library.

Library of Congress Catalog Card Number: on file.

Paperback ISBN 978 1 473 60009 6

eBook ISBN 978 1 473 60011 9

10 9 8 7 6 5 4 3 2 1

The publisher has used its best endeavours to ensure that any website addresses referred to in this book are correct and active at the time of going to press. However, the publisher and the author have no responsibility for the websites and can make no guarantee that a site will remain live or that the content will remain relevant, decent or appropriate.

The publisher has made every effort to mark as such all words which it believes to be trademarks. The publisher should also like to make it clear that the presence of a word in the book, whether marked or unmarked, in no way affects its legal status as a trademark.

Every reasonable effort has been made by the publisher to trace the copyright holders of material in this book. Any errors or omissions should be notified in writing to the publisher, who will endeavour to rectify the situation for any reprints and future editions.

Typeset by Cenveo® Publisher Services.

Printed and bound in Great Britain by CPI Group (UK) Ltd., Croydon, CR0 4YY.

John Murray Learning policy is to use papers that are natural, renewable and recyclable products and made from wood grown in sustainable forests. The logging and manufacturing processes are expected to conform to the environmental regulations of the country of origin.

John Murray Learning
338 Euston Road
London NW1 3BH
www.hodder.co.uk

Also available
in ebook

CONTENTS

This SECRETS book contains a number of special textual features, which have been developed to help you navigate the chapters quickly and easily. Throughout the book, you will find these indicated by the following icons.

 Each chapter contains **quotes** from inspiring figures. These will be useful for helping you understand different viewpoints and why each Secret is useful in a practical context.

 Also included in each chapter are a number of **strategies** that outline techniques for putting this Secret into practice.

 The **putting it all together** box at the end of each chapter provides a summary of each chapter, and a quick way into the core concepts of each Secret.

12
13
(14)
15

You'll also see a **chapter ribbon** down the right hand side of each right-hand page, to help you mark your progress through the book and to make it easy to refer back to a particular chapter you found useful or inspiring.

INTRODUCTION

There's no doubt about it, a happy relationship feels good and is life-enhancing. We are likely to be happier as individuals too and to enjoy better health. We don't, of course, necessarily need to be in a relationship to be happy – lots of us are happy as singletons. But a happy relationship is the thoroughly beneficial icing on the cake of a happy life and many find that, for them, being in a good relationship is essential to their overall happiness.

The first key to a good relationship is love. It's love that turns an attraction or mutual likeability into the wish to spend more time together. It is love that helps you make the decision to commit to each other exclusively. It is love that encourages you to live together. It is love that gives you the feeling that you want to love each other forever, and in good faith promise each other that you will.

At the beginning, when you're first together, the wonderful feeling of being 'in love' is totally spontaneous. You feel like dancing and just about every aspect of life seems brighter. The happiness of love infuses you and seems to be all around, just like in the song lyrics!

Love may arrive quickly, indeed almost instantly, when mutual attraction and like ability fuse in a breathtaking kind of wonder. Or it may develop gradually until the growing friendship blossoms into full love.

However this amazing rapport comes about, every in-love couple assumes it will always be like this and can't imagine not loving each other and being happy together. You think your love will last for ever.

Sadly this often isn't the case and the reality is very different. In more than 20 years as a relationship therapist I've counselled countless couples whose love had faded and sometimes died. One in two marriages ends in divorce and a far higher proportion of unmarried couples break up. Then there are the countless couples who opt to stay together even though one or both partners are unhappy.

So what goes wrong?

The fundamental problem is a general misconception that love is unconditional and a belief or vain hope that, along with mutual attraction, it will last forever of its own accord. Then, when this belief proves wrong and love dims or disappears, the couple find themselves unequipped to resolve the mounting difficulties or apathy between them. Unaddressed or mishandled the problems only grow until one or both partners reach a place where they believe their only options are to either endure the ensuing unhappiness in which they find themselves, or separate. In this manner the love that held so much promise and beauty, uncared for in the way it needs, withers or disintegrates.

Is it possible to avoid this happening and for love to keep flourishing? Absolutely!

Love can and often does last a lifetime and I've made it my life's mission as a therapist and agony aunt to help couples who essentially love each other and deeply want their relationship to be happy and to continue living harmoniously together to realize their desire for lasting love.

For it isn't just a dream or a chance happening – it truly can be a chosen reality. When I talk to happy couples I am always struck by the strength and steadfastness of their love and basically contented togetherness. Yes, most of them, for sure, have their ups and downs but through them all they nevertheless continue to love and cherish each other and are ready, always, to adjust their particular way of togetherness so that they stay on parallel tracks even when they're not quite on the same one.

Just as there are numerous problems that a couple may have, there are plentiful solutions to avoid or remedy them and all sorts of ways to encourage and enable lasting love and happiness. Ask any happy couple the secret of their long-term love and they will give you any one of a myriad answers since every relationship is different. But over the years I've realized that the countless small individual secrets of happiness fall under the umbrella of the 50 Secrets of Happy Relationships in this book. Each of the Secrets is intrinsically therapeutic, soothing, constructive and energizing.

Brilliantly, each of them is also essentially easy to understand and use, and each of them, as both partners integrate them in their day-to-day lives, not only heals and helps enable love to keep thriving, but feels good in itself.

Each of the Secrets is autonomously and intrinsically vital to relationship happiness and while each Secret is beneficial and transformational in its own right, they work together harmoniously and interdependently too. They often have similar characteristics and elements and so merge into each other seamlessly or weave in and out of each other in a complementary rapport.

While the Secrets might address problems that are current in your relationship or that could arise, they are good to read and inspiring as their focus is on living happily together and dealing successfully with any actual or potential difficulties. It may be about living together peacefully and interacting in a way that means you avoid problems in the first place or pre-empt any that may be possible or are already threatening. Alternatively where there are existing issues, choosing a solution-oriented attitude as you activate and action the Secret.

Lasting happiness is inherently dependent on our understanding how to live in a way that allows and enables us to be happy and on choosing to live this way now and throughout our life. While our genes, upbringing and experiences can give us a propensity to be more or less happy than others, we are also given the ability to work around these influences, choose a positive attitude to life and forge happiness for ourselves in spite of any negative influences and in addition to benign ones. It's especially true of relationship happiness, for if you have a partner not only do you have your own happiness to think of but each other's, and you bring two lots of genes and other influences to your togetherness.

Self and mutual understanding is a huge help in nurturing your self-confidence to find and maintain happiness both individually and as a couple.

The importance of understanding the cause and effect of happiness in every aspect of your relationship and in all the phases and stages of your life together comes up again and again throughout the Secrets as does your power to choose to know and use the Secrets and to live happily together.

Relationship happiness, once you're through the initial heady phase of spontaneous early attraction, is all about looking after your love by behaving in ways that demonstrate you treasure each other and the love you share.

In so doing, the two of you have inestimable power to influence the way your relationship works and your happiness together. For, like so much in our lives, you'll find the dynamic between you is based on the cause and effect you both generate with your actions.

You can't 'make' each other happy, of course, for to a great extent we each hold our happiness in our hands, but you can choose to have a positive attitude, to do everything in your power not to make each other unhappy and to generate and maintain an interaction that is a vibrant, loving measure of your regard for each other.

And there you step into the magic of happiness that comes from knowing and incorporating into your life and love together the Secrets of happy relationships and the strategies for staying in love.

You will find you know many of them already – perhaps all of them – and yet it's so easy to forget their huge importance. This book isn't only about learning them – it's also about remembering them! Loyalty, trust, kindness and respect, for instance, are integral to any friendship and never more so than within a romantic relationship. The more you think about it, the more you will see how incredibly important they are to continuing to like and love each other.

And yet our busy lives, together with complacency and belief in the myth that love is always spontaneous, can conspire to cause couples to neglect caring for each other's wellbeing and the love they share. They then slide into a carelessness that morphs quickly into a kind of disrespect – sometimes one-sided as the other struggles to make up for it, sometimes mutual.

The longer this carelessness and disrespect continues, the more problems arise. A couple may not register how unhappy their relationship has become. Then one day one or other will realize that they are no longer happy together and, often only gradually, the realization comes that they are in fact unhappy. It's usually only at this point that a couple seeks help. If it's not too late – if they still love each other to some extent – and they have the wish and will to revitalize their love, they can learn or remember the Secrets and bring them back into practice in their relationship again.

The Secrets' healing and regenerative power can transform even a seriously ailing relationship – I've seen it happen many times. Even if one or both partners has lost their love and/ or their inclination to bring it back to the relationship it is not necessarily too late. If they decide to give the Secrets a chance and put their all into helping them work, they can again bring about a positive turnaround. From unhappiness to happiness the Secrets take your lives and your interaction in hand and guide you back to full-on love and caring tenderness. It feels like magic. It isn't – it's cause and effect – practical, constructive, powerful and transforming. There is indeed a catalytic ingredient in all this, though. It's the energy and spirit of love and all it needs is your attention and your spirit and it can thrive, and last for ever.

You are reading this book and so I know that you are alert to the danger of being complacent about or neglectful of the love you and your partner share. And there is still love between you, or you would not be prepared to put in the effort to cherish it now and on an ongoing basis.

Keep love in your heart as you read this book. Let this love and the power of your mind guide you to recognize which Secrets or which part of a Secret strike a particular chord with your relationship.

Don't be alarmed if something you read makes you feel discomfited or angry or sad. Take a look at the uncomfortable feeling with all your honesty and insight. When faced, negative feelings can be revealing and enlightening. Learn about the feeling and its relevance to yourself and your partner and the way you interact. Getting to the core of relationship difficulties enables you to start resolving them. Recognizing ill feeling is the first step towards healing it.

Use this book. It can't of itself transform a lack or deficit of love to a blissful lovingness between you but it can show all kinds of ways to help love to last and flourish, some of which will be good for your particular personalities and your unique relationship.

Use it with love in your hearts. Use it together – for love takes two.

Remember also that love and togetherness and rapport are all based on a positive attitude that believes in them, supports them and engenders a kindness to each other. Being kind is not about patronizing or being falsely nice to each other. It is about being thoughtful, caring, encouraging and not just willing but enthusiastic about engaging with each other. It is a quality that feels good to experience in every way. It is a quality in a happy relationship that can make it sparkle with joy, flirt again with desire, share laughter, resonate with contentment. All the Secrets have their own kind of power that seems equally miraculous and is. They all support and enable love. Love itself is miraculous because looked after it thrives and looks after you.

Live the miracle. It is yours to spark, yours to continue. Cherish each other throughout your life together. Believe in love and never stop believing. Love is within you and all around you and the Secrets are always at hand to keep your love flourishing. I wish you both joy.

Relish the scope and diversity of love

> *'Being deeply loved by someone gives you strength, while loving someone deeply gives you courage.'* Laozi

> *'Where there is love there is life.'* Mohandas Gandhi

> *'Affection is responsible for nine-tenths of whatever solid and durable happiness there is in our lives.'* C. S. Lewis

> *'Love is a force more formidable than any other. It is invisible – it cannot be seen or measured, yet it is powerful enough to transform you in a moment, and offer you more joy than any material possession could.'* Barbara De Angelis

> *'What we have once enjoyed we can never lose. All that we love deeply becomes a part of us.'* Helen Keller

Love, in every relationship, is a special, living thing. It has a pulse, a spirit, a unique personality. Above all, it gives you a huge capacity for mutual happiness and often joy, for companionship, inspiration, support.

And all it takes for it to thrive is for you and your partner to appreciate it.

Just think, this moment, what a happy, loving relationship, ideally, means to you. Jot down the first things that come into your head. Now ask your partner and your friends what they think. What does it mean to them?

Instantly, you've realized some of the vast potential when two people love each other. And your relationship and the love you feel belongs to the two of you. It's completely yours. Isn't that amazingly inspiring?

I mentioned this to a friend and she said: 'To me it's daunting — it's such a responsibility! Relationships aren't easy — they're hard work. And anyway, what is love?'

Yes, there are two ways of looking at it: you too could choose to regard it as hard work, a heavy responsibility and pressure and to be sceptical about romantic love.

Or — and this is the very first secret of a happy relationship — you can choose to view it instead as inspirational, promising, a wonderful opportunity. This way you open up the whole universe of your relationship to its full potential and a happiness that weaves through not only your togetherness but also enriches your individual lives.

It's something you choose to create — every moment, every day. And recognition of this potential is all it takes to activate positivity and happiness.

There are so many things you each bring to your togetherness, so many ways you can gently steer it as you both wish, ways you can grow it, ways you can enjoy it, ways you can use this amazing opportunity to enhance your happiness — and that's your individual happiness as well as your happiness together. For they are inclusive of each other: when your relationship is happy, you are each more likely to be happy as an individual. When you are happy in your individual selves, your relationship together is more likely to be happy. The different aspects of our happiness and love work together.

This Secret dusts all the other secrets and your whole relationship with gold.

TREAT EVERY DAY AS A NEW DAY

Treat every day as a new day in your relationship — a new beginning. When you wake up in the morning, take a moment to be aware of the scope of your relationship. Let the wonder of the diversity of love and togetherness and the potential for happiness flow over you. Realize, too, that your relationship is yours to guide positively in your own way, this day and every day.

Now relish the scope this gives you to get on well and to let your love blossom.

Imagine that you are ideally placed to realize the possibilities of your relationship. Imagine you can suddenly see clearly the potential the two of you have to have a wonderful time, together, now and into the future.

Understand and believe that this is now your reality – a reality of your making. Remember it's in your hands – your absolute control, the two of you together – to look after your togetherness as you move through your lives. Decide that you will care for your love – and enjoy it to the full.

Bask in the knowledge that the two of you are setting out on one of the most fulfilling journeys. No matter how happy together you've been – or indeed unhappy – from now on you are going to not just realize the scope you share but use the spirit of the joyous life-force of love that you create together, to live to the full your truly happy relationship.

LET GO OF NEGATIVE THOUGHTS AND CHOOSE TO THINK POSITIVELY

Remember that to create positivity in the present you need to and can let go of any negativity that's hanging around from the last few days, months and years. Deliberately choose instead to think and feel positively and lovingly. If uncomfortable or painful memories and feelings pop up, remember the notes you made just now on an ideal relationship. Think how you can maximize the lovely parts that already exist, right now, between you and then focus on others you'd like to bring into being.

Remember that feeling happy and loving isn't necessarily spontaneous. Certainly it can be, especially in the early days when you're 'in love'. But, mostly, happiness and love are feelings we consciously invite into our lives, open ourselves up to and look after with kindness and all sorts of other loving behaviour that we'll be looking at throughout the Secrets.

Now decide how you personally can apply some of these caring, loving elements in your relationship today. A good start, for most of us, is to aim to be pleasant to your partner at all times. Firmly decide not to snap or be rude in any other way. Also to guard against criticizing, pressing their buttons, putting them down. Decide to be actively supportive, kind, encouraging, full of praise for their good points and actions.

Think, too, how good it will feel to be your best self around them – kind, loving and caring. To smile instead of scowling, to think positive thoughts instead of grumbling, and to embrace life instead of fighting it – and your partner. We can't always change our circumstances but by choosing to behave lovingly we allow love in – and it can be astonishingly powerful.

LET LOVE GUIDE YOU IN MAKING PROGRESS

We progress through each day in a series of moments, phases and steps. Each part of the day, everything that happens, every action and even every opportunity to quietly think is an opportunity to let love guide you.

Being aware of love in all its diversity will enable you to stop negative reactions to your partner in their tracks and replace them with a chosen positivity. You'll see clearly and immediately that you really do make your own reality in your relationship just as you do in every part of your life.

Don't worry if you can't think of hundreds of ways to be loving just now – as you move through the book or dip into the Secrets you will discover a myriad diverse ways to let love flow through your relationship, washing it with loving feelings and happiness.

Putting it all together

When you make it your practice to appreciate and relish the tremendous scope of love to make your relationship not just a comfortable place to be but a joyous and happy one, you pave the way to letting love in to every area of your relationship. You'll find it has a knock-on effect on your whole life, which in turn makes it easier to be loving and caring in your relationship.

Every single time you choose to think how you can react to them with love in your heart and to do the loving thing, you will find that you have a beneficial effect on what's happening around you both, and how you and your partner are getting on.

When you choose to be loving to your partner in a wide variety of ways, throughout the day, actively refusing to be churlish or unkind and choosing instead to be caring and thoughtful and to cherish them, you nurture the love between you, enabling it to thrive and blossom.

Realizing the diversity and scope of love and your part in letting them flourish is the first step to learning all the Secrets of Happy Relationships.

And it feels wonderful.

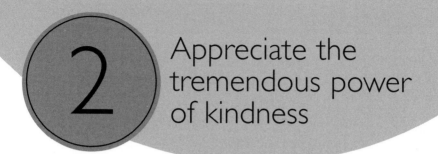

2 Appreciate the tremendous power of kindness

'Unexpected kindness is the most powerful, least costly and most underrated agent of human change.' Bob Kerrey

'A tree is known by its fruit; a man by his deeds. A good deed is never lost; he who sows courtesy reaps friendship, and he who plants kindness gathers love.'
St Basil, Bishop of Caesarea

'I have never met a person whose greatest need was anything other than real, unconditional love. You can find it in a simple act of kindness towards someone who needs help. There is no mistaking love... it is the common fibre of life, the flame that heats our soul, energizes our spirit and supplies passion to our lives.' Elisabeth Kübler-Ross

'Self-esteem is very fragile and gets pounded by so many forces outside the relationship that it's all the more important to feel appreciated by the most significant person in your life.'
Peggy & James Vaughan

'Real love always creates, it never destroys.' Leo Buscaglia

Kindness is a powerful catalyst in happiness and never more so than in a relationship.

Yet there is a curious dichotomy in life today: we're often urged, very wisely, to be caring and compassionate, yet there are some people who are intent on making kindness out to be silly and sissy and who also equally mistakenly believe that sarcasm and other kinds of unkindness are cool.

The truth is that if you are kind to each other you give your relationship the very best chance to flourish. Kindness – and that's any and every act of kindness as well as a generally kind attitude – creates a climate of goodwill that passes back and forth between you and draws you together. Importantly, too, it's an instant reminder that you love each other – for how easy it is to forget this in the hustle and bustle of life!

Like love, kindness feels good in both the giving and the receiving, and it's essential food for love between the two of you.

Like love again, being kind has a big influence on all parts of life. If you start the day by being thoughtful of your partner's wellbeing and actively promoting it by being kind, you set yourself up, as well as them, to go out into the day with a warm heart. Whatever happens at work, you'll both be more inclined to interact positively with others. Kindness, like love, ripples out from one person to another to another and at the same time stays with you, giving you an inner glow.

Kindness has a mirror effect, just as unkindness does. Snap at your partner and they'll snap back or feel dejected. So you've created a pool of unhappiness that taints the moment and perhaps the whole day. Say or do something nice for them and they'll be pleased and almost certainly want to please you too.

Being kind feels good, too, and even if it's rebuffed by your partner it may in time help restore their equilibrium and happiness. It's feel good healing in action.

EACH DAY RESOLVE TO BE KIND

Every day make a resolution to be kind. Just thinking of the myriad random ways you can be kind to and with your partner will give you a warm feeling and make you feel well-disposed to them, even if you didn't already. It is so simple yet demonstrably effective. Your partner will appreciate anything you do that's kind. Even if they don't respond actively with thanks or even acknowledgement, they will take in what you've done or how you're being and it will have a positive effect for kindness is inherently positive. It feels good to give and receive and you'll automatically feel more loving and happier towards each other.

Have a think, too, about how you can keep in a kind frame of mind towards them throughout the day. As in the first Secret of relishing the scope and diversity of love, take a moment to take pleasure in anticipating how it will feel to behave kindly to your partner throughout the day ahead. Ask yourself 'How will it feel not to ignore him, or to be in any way negatively critical of him in my own mind or in conversation with him or any of my friends?' Doesn't it feel worlds better than not being kind?

EXPERIENCE HOW GOOD IT FEELS TO BE KIND

Consider your ability to be kind just as precious as winning the lottery – not only does it make you feel happy but it stands to give you a happy relationship. Have fun deciding what you'd like to do in terms of kindness and how it will feel to you and your partner. Just as it's fun to imagine what you'd give to others if you won the lottery, imagine what kindnesses you can give your partner which, though free, will be hugely precious in their own way. Perhaps you're thinking: 'I'd have to be a saint and I'm not' You don't have to be a saint or even an especially good or nice person to be kind. Like most skills in life, being generous with kindness improves and gets easier the more you do it. At first, it may seem like an awful lot of effort to do kind things, whether large or small. You may think 'I haven't got time to mess about!' But this is about the happiness of your relationship – one of the most important things in your life – probably the most important. So make time and decide to put in the effort.

MAKE KINDNESS YOUR HABIT

Develop a kind attitude. Kindness isn't a one-off, random act of kindness – it's an attitude and a habit. Like any other talent – and you have the talent so rejoice! – it's up to you to use it regularly and thoughtfully and lovingly. Be kind throughout the day. Be kind even if you've got a headache or some other pain or discomfort. Be kind even if you've had a difficult time at work. Be kind even if your partner isn't being kind to you.

And respond kindly to your partner's words and actions. For instance, if your partner says something, listen and take an interest. Tell them something about yourself and your day too. Share thoughts with each other. This is kindness in action and it's hugely powerful in creating a fair balance between the two of you that not only feels comfortable but keeps the happiness that flows between you level – and that's on a high level. Be aware of the difference it makes between you and give thanks for it. Remember how good it felt for both of you. Reflect that you don't have to win the lottery – you are winning treasures immeasurable in terms of your relationship's happiness when you are kind.

Putting it all together

Kindness always feels good. Not that that's why we should be kind, of course – we are kind to help others feel good and to help in some way to make their life run more easily and happily. But it's lovely that it also feels good to us. And once again, because your mood will effortlessly lift when you're kind – or even, as you're already finding, just in thinking about being kind – you'll be lovely to be around and easy to get on with.

All you have to do is remember. Even the sweetest-natured people can be grumpy and edgy if they feel out of sorts or mix with other spiky or doleful people. But all it takes is a second to catch yourself before you say something unkind or do something selfish. In that second you can turn around your action or reaction and choose – and it is a choice, your choice, every step of the way – to instead say something kind and do something that shows you care.

That's all it takes. A moment's thought followed by a decision to choose the kind way.

It will transform the moments – all the moments – from potentially unhappy to a positive, kind-centred zone. Kindness enables you, your partner and your relationship to be in a positive vibe – a good place.

You create kindness. Kindness creates a good place to be. Let kindness be the home of your relationship.

3 Communicate

66 *'Much unhappiness has come into the world because of bewilderment and things left unsaid.'* Fyodor Dostoyevsky

66 *'The single biggest problem with communication is the illusion that it has taken place.'* George Bernard Shaw

66 *'A beautiful thing happens when we start paying attention to each other. It is by participating more in your relationship that you breathe life into it.'* Dr Steve Maraboli

66 *'Sometimes, reaching out and taking someone's hand is the beginning of a journey. At other times, it is allowing another to take yours.'* Vera Nazarian

66 *'Having not said anything the first time, it was somehow even more difficult to broach the subject the second time around.'* Douglas Adams

It's hugely important that you communicate well with each other. For how can you know each other if you don't tell each other who you are? How can you each know, if you don't tell each other clearly, what the other is thinking and how they're feeling?

And as we forget, and change, and stubbornly like to think we know what perhaps we don't know, we need to keep sharing information about ourselves throughout our time together, throughout our lives, so that we do know something of how and who we are, today.

At the beginning of relationships we talk and talk and give of ourselves in other ways too, generously and abundantly. But talking intimately is a learning curve for most of us and once past the in-love early phase when we want to be so deeply connected we're almost inside each other's heads, the spontaneous impulse to connect intimately lessens or even disappears. We need to choose to talk and to let each other in on how we're feeling, what's going on in our lives and, so importantly, on our current ideas, aspirations, ambitions and aims.

It is of course quite possible to get by in a relationship without talking much personally. But for the active, thriving happiness that you're seeking you'll want to know each other – only then can you truly love each other, for anything less is a mirage. How can it be love of the real you if you haven't enabled your partner to know the real you and vice versa?

As with most of the Secrets, we get better at talking and other forms of communication, the more we do it. It becomes clearer and deeper and as we give out information about ourselves, we learn about ourselves. One of the most illuminating ways to learn more about yourselves is to talk with each other. It's essential this is a two-way thing – and for that you need mutual trust and an understanding that this is what you both want.

Mutual understanding is the essence of a relationship. As you relate to each other intentionally and meaningfully, so you engage, involving each other in your individual lives and your life together, and actively participating in the love you constantly look after and renew.

PRACTISE TALKING

Consider the ways in which you share information about yourself with your partner. Talking is usually the major channel for our thoughts and feelings. But do you talk with each other as much as you used to? Do you share generously your current ideas and feelings and listen to his? Is it a habit you've lost in the hustle and bustle of jobs, families, leisure activities and looking after your friendships? Since childhood you've probably been taught to watch what you say to avoid offending others, which is sensible but can go too far – many get so good at not saying what they want that in the end they lose the art of openness and honesty. But all it takes is a willingness to practise talking – really meaningfully talking – again with your partner.

So agree to practise. Your partner will almost certainly be glad that you want to. Help each other. Remember that conversation is like tennis – you take turns. When it's their turn, don't disengage by thinking of what you're going to say next, listen intently with your full attention. Remind them, if their mind wanders, to do the same for you. It may be necessary to remind each other gently – with a smile in your eyes as well as your voice – that it isn't about either or both of you holding the floor for hours. All conversation usually takes is turns of a minute or two.

SHOW YOUR INTEREST IN EACH OTHER'S WORDS

Help each other talk in as many ways as you can. Your body language is key. If they look at you as they talk, meet their eyes. Show you're 'receiving' them by acknowledging what they say – maybe with an 'mmm' or a 'that's interesting' or 'I didn't know that'. Use your facial expressions too to convey your interest and empathy with, or at least an understanding of, what they're trying to say. And ask questions – it's so easy to misunderstand, so check your understanding is correct and be happy to elucidate or re-cap if they ask you something. And don't be impatient about repetition. Remember that if we repeat something it's probably because we need to. Talk about it rather than being impatient.

Don't always multitask when you're talking – it can be a menace to good communication as real engagement needs to be focused, one on one. I know that with our busy lives, we're used to doing lots of things at once, but it's essential to pause and have some genuine one-to-one time with each other at least once every day. Make it a priority. Remember that your relationship is **very, very** important to you both – cherish it by actively putting aside special time just for the two of you to genuinely communicate.

And delight in it. It's so good to have someone in your life who is there for you and you for them and who you can relate to and share thoughts and this expression of love with.

Pay attention to each other – it's the best gift you can give each other and yourselves.

COMMUNICATE IN OTHER WAYS TOO

As well as talking, there are many other ways to connect intimately even when you're with others and/or multitasking. Be aware of them. Let them know you're thinking of them by distilling your thoughts and feelings in small actions that might go unnoticed by anyone else. Catch their eyes and smile, for instance; laugh generously at each other's jokes, even if you've heard them a million times; give them a look of love, touch their hand or shoulder gently – all these are potent carriers of information that you approve of, like and love them. It is the little acknowledgements that you are close to them and delight in these seemingly small moments of connection that mean so much. Like young lovers, leave each other notes in unexpected places. You can also invent personal signals that transmit a message without anyone else knowing – that's fun and it again draws you close. And every day remember to use the Secret 2 in a series of kindnesses throughout the day. It's a potent sign that you are paying attention to each other and love pleasing your partner. And remember, too, that all-important kiss and hug whenever you take your leave of each other and meet up again. They are small gestures but so very meaningful and important.

Putting it all together

Be gentle with each other as you talk, generous in what you share, above all interested. It's a wonderful Secret – once you're in the habit it's fun and enlightening and, most important of all, it draws you close.

The wonderful thing is the attention you're giving each other. It's love in action and makes you both feel good.

Talking and all other kinds of communication enable connection, understanding and closeness on an ongoing basis. Through them you nurture your early rapport and deep liking and love for each other and carry it, strong and rich, throughout your relationship as the years go by.

Choose to relish it as one of life's greatest pleasures. It is!

Don't take everything personally

❝ *'Let your intention be freedom from useless suffering. Then, let go.'* Elizabeth Gilbert

❝ *'Lift up the self by the self*
And don't let the self drop down
For the self is the self's only friend
And the self is the self's only foe.' Bhagavad Gita

❝ *'Don't take anything personally. Nothing others do is because of you. What others say and do is a projection of their own reality, their own dream. When you are immune to the opinions and actions of others, you won't be the victim of needless suffering.'* Miguel Ruiz

❝ *'When someone says something to you, whether it be an insult, piece of advice, or anything at all, connect back to your awareness. Only you can know what is true or not. By taking another person's opinion of yourself to heart and choosing to believe it, you are doing yourself a huge injustice.'* Jackie Vecchio

❝ *'It isn't always about you.'* Rosie Hallett

It's all too easy to confuse this very natural wish with the spurious idea that you are 'making' them happy, and they you. For no one can make anyone else happy on the personal inner happiness front. Their happiness is largely dependent on their positivity and their chosen attitude. And no one can be totally responsible for another's bad moods – it's up to each of us how we react. Yet because we're brought up to please others, it's very easy to get anxious and fret that we've somehow upset them and that it must all be our fault. 'Is everything all right?' you probably ask. 'What's wrong?' And if your partner says: 'Yes I'm fine,' although they clearly aren't, and 'Nothing's wrong,' when it clearly is, we worry even more that we're the cause of it.

Of course there may be times when their bad mood is directly linked to you and then you'll need to encourage them to talk to you about it. But it's vital to remember that your partner's feelings don't solely revolve around you and that there are myriad reasons for fits of the blues or grouchiness that may have nothing whatsoever to do with you. When this is the case, probing and fussing over them and fretting about what you can have done to cause this are no help at all. In fact, the more you show your concern, the more it may seem like you're nagging them and that could exacerbate their bad mood. It might also activate a pernicious cycle of control if they see they have the power to manipulate your emotions so easily. Or it might simply add worry about the effect they're having on you to the weight of their current low period.

By realizing that their down time isn't because of you, you free them to recover their equilibrium of their own accord, while you maintain your own balance and happiness.

DON'T ASSUME RESPONSIBILITY FOR YOUR PARTNER'S MOOD

The minute you notice that your partner seems low or grouchy and sense you are in danger of his negativity affecting you, remember that his mood may have nothing to do with you. Assess the circumstances. Is this a familiar occurrence with him – perhaps at this particular time of day – or forming another pattern? If so, realize that this is not your story and let them take responsibility for their mood and deal with it and come through it in their own way and time. Remember that even if they are focusing their anger or other negativity on you, you do not have to take it on board. A counselling friend of mine, whose work meant he would sometimes be verbally attacked by clients trying to transfer onto him their anger at someone or something in their life, would effectively deal with it by saying to himself and them: 'I do not have to accept this.' It holds up a mirror and often stops the verbal attack in its tracks. Another way is to say: 'I'm sorry you are feeling low, but please don't direct it onto me.' If there is a pattern, point it out, gently of course and not in any way blaming or shaming. Help constructively if you can (see below).

RECOGNIZE THE POSSIBLE CAUSE OF MOODS

Take a daily situation that causes a lot of difficulty between a couple: tiredness. Your partner comes in from work, for instance, and, having been firing on all cylinders all day, in the comfort of your home suddenly slumps with fatigue. It's a common happening with those whose body clock has a natural blip at around 6 in the evening and it's often exacerbated by low blood sugar in the run up to an evening meal. They literally feel like growling and are liable to snap at anyone in their vicinity – and of course that just happens to be you. But actually their low has nothing whatsoever to do with you. They may just need half an hour's quiet rest or other relaxation to unwind and you can help by making sure they have it. If your meal together is some way off, a quick energy-boosting snack will restore their energy and good mood. Be warm and kind and don't fuss or respond negatively.

TAKE CARE OF YOUR OWN EQUILIBRIUM

Remind yourself to look after your own positivity and equilibrium with tender loving care. No one else can sabotage them if you don't allow them to. If your feelings are ruffled or you sense in any way that you are receiving your partner's negativity, take time out to go to a quiet place in your mind and, if possible, out of their vicinity. Meditate and/or breathe slowly and deeply, telling yourself that you are not to blame for their upset and inviting peace and calm to stay with you.

Choose a phrase that you like, to remind yourself that you are a lovely, kind person and want to live positively and happily and are prepared to deal with relationship difficulties constructively when the need arises.

Use one of the quotes at the beginning of this Secret to remind yourself that you are not personally responsible for other people's moods.

Putting it all together

Happy relationships take two, but each individual person is responsible for their own positivity and happiness. When you both respect each other's autonomy as far as feelings and moods are concerned, you enable each other to find the solutions constructively, taking responsibility for them yourselves. You neither let yourself feel responsible for your partner's moods, nor expect them to feel they are the cause of yours.

With self and mutual respect, you allow each other to grow and learn and you nurture the happiness of your relationship free of over-dependence on each other.

5 Live and love in the present

❝ *'Love is continually engaged in the process of opening new doors and windows so that fresh ideas and questions can be admitted.'* Leo Buscaglia

❝ *'The past has no power over the present moment.'* Eckhart Tolle

❝ *'To live in the present, you need to act or accept but never stay stuck.'* John Kuypers

❝ *'You should start where you are.'* Ruth Ozeki

❝ *'You have a clean slate, and you can start over – right here, right now. Find your joy and live it!'* Rhonda Byrne

We all have baggage – it comes with life and sticks to us like a limpet if we let it. But, happily, we don't have to. Your experiences are yours to dwell on, or not, as you wish for even the kind of unpleasant, pernicious memories that crop up in flashbacks post-traumatically can be refused entry to our current happiness, or prospect of happiness. But the Secret of living happily together in the present is to focus on how you both are, individually and together, right now and decide firmly not to let bad feelings from past relationships – and that includes the past of the one you're now in – sabotage your potential for present and future happiness.

Life is now. This moment, this day. It is all we can be sure of. It is yours to enjoy to the best of your ability and your ability is great. Living positively and being aware of the love in your own soul and all around you is a choice you make now and can continue to make as the years roll by. And roll by they will, faster than you can imagine, so it's vital to catch the moment and love, love, love with all your heart and mind and spirit.

The past and future can be your allies in this. By learning from past experiences you can help guide a positive approach for the two of you together now. By remembering the good parts, you can light up each new day with them. By proactively deciding to avoid re-creating past mistakes in the future and choosing to use the Secrets instead, you create happiness as your lives together unfold.

LIVE IN THE PRESENT, NOT THE PAST

Refuse to allow the past to irrelevantly cause trouble in the present. You can't stop memories popping into your mind, but you can prevent them from staying there. The first key to living and loving in the moment is to declutter your mind of recurring thoughts and feelings from past bad experiences. It's necessary to make another decision but as with all the other decisions you'll be taking throughout the series of Secrets, it's one that is surprisingly easy to make. Putting it into action is easy too, but first you need to realize that allowing the past to invade and sabotage your present is a habit you don't have to subscribe to. Awareness of this is like an invisible protector through which no nasty memories and feelings that have no relevance today can penetrate.

All it takes to don this protector is to notice the minute you are tenser than a situation merits. Noticing you are overreacting to your partner's behaviour is half the battle in letting go of the tension, which not only will be helpful in resolving the issue but may simply dissolve it immediately.

CONCENTRATE ON MAKING EACH DAY A GOOD ONE

Think of it as a blank canvas, and you and your partner the artists who are going to create a picture of life that is enjoyable and beautiful for you both. You are free to put in this picture whatever you want, in the way you want. Think of painting in love and compatibility, enjoyment of each other's company, harmony not conflict, and mutual support and appreciation rather than maliciousness and discord.

Decide now that this is what you want, adding any other positive attributes of the relationship you want to share as they come to mind. Jot them down. This note-taking helps in many of the Secrets and is as beneficial in this one as the others. (Jotting them down in your memory is fine if you're not the kind of person who'd rather do it with pen and paper.)

Have fun thinking of the picture you want to create together. Notice I don't say 'would like to create' – 'want' is strong and certain. Really want, passionately want, to paint a brilliant happy relationship that will enhance your lives. It is yours for the wanting. It is yours now if it is what you both truly, passionately want. It is yours now to create.

Believe in it, and you are already in it.

LIVE POSITIVELY, CONSTRUCTIVELY AND INSPIRINGLY

The present is what matters. You've learned how to oust the habit of letting uncomfortable memories sabotage your current relationship. Similarly, beware letting worries about what may or may not happen in the future affect your happiness today.

Life and love is about what's happening now. The present and future are yours to manage and steer. It is up to you to decide how you react to current aspects of your life together, and which way you go forwards.

Use what you've learned from the past to help you go forwards in your path beneficially. Harness your common sense and wisdom, too, to make decisions, for instance on when it's best to accept things as they are and when you need to make changes. Be very active in being loving and pleasant to each other and generally as good-natured and caring as your best self.

Whether it's acceptance or change that's needed, act positively, seeing the good there is and bringing love into every move you make, relishing the many blessings you have, appreciating each other to the full.

Wisdom helps you make the present better. Use it. Love it. Love yourselves, each other and your relationship now and happiness is yours. And it is now.

Putting it all together

Steadfastly live in the moment – within yourself, your life, all your dealings with friends, family and colleagues and, most of all, within your relationship. Concentrate on where you are now, this minute, and do whatever you can to make it positive, good, loving. You can't wave a magic wand and change your partner, if they are set on being stuck in some kind of negative trough, but you can change your being – that is, your attitude to them and to your present generally. As you do so you will inevitably change the dynamic between you, enabling your partner to adapt to positivity in some way. (See Secret 36: Take your tiger to the mountain.)

It's as though positivity lets the light in, illuminating what's needed between you. Often, all that is needed is love. Not just a gesture of romance or appreciation, good though that is, but a simple willingness to smooth your hackles and in the process, probably theirs.

The effect of living in the moment is, unsurprisingly, immediate. And it's powerful. Focusing on now, you bring all your energy and goodness and love and wisdom and common sense to the occasion. You turn towards each other instead of away. You enable yourselves, in that moment, to be nice to each other.

Forget the past. Don't fret about the future. The one is gone and done with. The other will take care of itself, in time. All you and your partner need to do is feel and appreciate your togetherness now and in so doing you turn out the potential for discord, invite in harmony and enable your love to thrive.

6 Find empathy and compassion

'We think we listen, but very rarely do we listen with real understanding, true empathy. Yet listening, of this very special kind, is one of the most potent forces for change that I know.' Carl Rogers

'You never really understand a person until you consider things from his point of view... until you climb into his skin and walk around in it.' Harper Lee in To Kill a Mockingbird

'Compassion turns you inside out and in the process you learn or remember to love.' Rosie Hallett

'Too often we underestimate the power of a touch, a smile, a kind word, a listening ear, an honest compliment, or the smallest act of caring, all of which have the potential to turn a life around.' Leo Buscaglia

'If you want others to be happy, practise compassion. If you want to be happy, practise compassion.' Dalai Lama

The Secrets work alongside each other in harmony, often overlapping and blending, and always helping each other. The combination of empathy and compassion is a prime catalyst in enabling all and any of the Secrets to let us stay happily in love.

One of the most powerful ways it protects the love between you is when one of you is about to embark on a blaming mission. But when we play the 'blame them, shame them' game we're on the road to dislike – and dislike is, no question, a killer of love. Stop, breathe and consider what your partner is feeling, and you'll instantly feel for them and with them. In this quantum leap you not only begin to understand them, but what's going on between you. Simultaneously that tension disappears. In so doing, you free the space for positive change – a shift in the dynamic between you, perhaps, that simply eases the difficulty, or a realization of a better way forward than carping and criticizing.

Compassion is simple – all it takes is to remember that your partner is a person much like you. They too have feelings, worries, doubts and insecurities. They too suffer from pride, bullheadedness and misjudgements. And they, like you, want to love and be loved. We all do. Remember that and you'll be compassionate. And when you are, it's one step into imagining yourself in their shoes and then you can feel what it's like to be them.

Perhaps more than anything else, compassion and empathy are at the core of love and happiness in relationships.

For two people living together very closely, hopefully for a long shared lifetime, they keep you in tandem – understanding, consoling, inspiring, healing and helping each other. Knowing that your partner feels for you and with you, you know they are rooting for you and want the very best for you. They help you to realize that you're not in competition with each other, but on the same side. When mutual compassion and empathy are strong, it's a fabulous feeling of mutual support and at the same time a tremendous strengthener to help each of you fly independently in the world along your own special flight path.

USE COMPASSION TO CREATE UNDERSTANDING AND ACCORD

To live together in accord, bring compassion into the equation. Sharing a relationship, you are going to encounter each other many times, every day. That could be being together in person, or on the phone or digitally. Every encounter is a chance for you both to react to each other, and every reaction brings emotions of one kind or another. It's very easy to get irritated or bored or to feel pressurized by your partner. But in any negative interaction, the simple act of reminding yourself about compassion is all it takes to turn it into a positive one. We've already looked (in Secret 4: Don't take everything personally) at how to avoid taking your partner's negativity on board or blaming yourself for it. Feeling with the person – feeling compassion – instantly puts you in their shoes or at least alongside them, rather than directly opposite them. You'll see then what's causing their behaviour and, in understanding it, you'll naturally simmer down. Then you can work together positively to sort out what needs to be done, or simply get on with your togetherness smoothly in an atmosphere of goodwill towards each other instead of the tension that was threatening.

TROUBLESHOOT YOUR EXASPERATION OR ANGER WITH COMPASSION AND EMPATHY

When discord hasn't just threatened but has descended on you both, big time, and you are about to launch into an attack or passively-aggressively withdraw, compassion and empathy are brilliant troubleshooters. The crucial element of this Secret is that you notice the minute you're about to jump into that blaming 'it's all your fault' cycle, and engage your brain. Then, instead, you hold back from the harsh or snide criticism you were about to vent, or just as perniciously sighing or tut-tutting impatiently, or seething quietly inside. Be very aware of how you are reacting and instead think quickly: 'Hey – this actually isn't all their fault.' It isn't. As we saw in Secret 4, grouchiness, yours or theirs, could be about your or their emotional baggage, or have a situational or physical cause. Pause to sense what's up with them and/or with you. You can use logic, common sense or simply intuit – give yourself the chance and you'll work out what's going on for you both in a couple of seconds. That's all it takes – a brief pause and compassion – feeling with them.

SHARE YOUR THOUGHTS AND FEELINGS READILY

It's very important for you and your partner to share your feelings with each other as this enables you to be as compassionate as possible. As important as listening is, it's just as vital to give them insights into your psyche by telling them about the emotional place you're in. You'll enable them to shift their attitude to you and to

25

feel compassion for you. Empathy often follows naturally, since it's surprising how often (when we understand what someone is going through) it echoes an experience we've had. In a relationship, the more you get to know each other and appreciate what you're each feeling and how you think about and react to things and why, the more easily you can step inside that individual's shoes and have a strong sense of how it feels to be them. Allowing your partner to understand you enables them to be compassionate towards you, just as you are to them, and the more compassion you share in your relationship, the more you'll be able to empathize with each other. Like all the Secrets, it feels good.

Putting it all together

It's very easy to lose our sympathy with each other and if we do we're likely pretty soon to lose our gentleness and this can sabotage our love for each other. Compassion holds hands with love. They are symbiotic in a good way, helping each other to grow and thrive. In the beginning of a relationship you spontaneously feel as though you are kindred spirits and you look for and find lots of ways to prove and show this. You like to show you feel for each other in the various trials and tribulations of life and often you try to genuinely empathize, feeling almost as strongly as though you are experiencing their experience yourself. As time goes by this doesn't happen so automatically – we regain our autonomy, which is perfectly healthy. But personal independence can co-exist with a deeply compassionate and empathic bond and when it does it enables you both to live happily on the individual front and as a couple. Most couples do care deeply for each other but forget to show it this way. Compassion isn't necessarily spontaneous – it's something you can remind yourself to feel for your partner, and empathy, too, is often down to letting yourself imagine what they are going through and be there with them, sharing their feelings and supporting them through. Compassion and empathy actively promote the continuation of the in-love feeling and at the same time help the deep love that matures throughout your relationship to keep blossoming forever. And it feels wonderful.

7 Affection is the greatest aphrodisiac

'Affection is responsible for nine-tenths of whatever solid and durable happiness there is in our lives.' C. S. Lewis

'It is the passion that is in a kiss that gives to it its sweetness; it is the affection in a kiss that sanctifies it.' Christian Nestell Bovee

'Caresses, expressions of one sort or another, are necessary to the life of the affections as leaves are to the life of a tree. If they are wholly restrained, love will die at the roots.' Nathaniel Hawthorne

'One of the best feelings in the world is when you hug someone you love and they hug you back even tighter.' Rick Warren

'Never leave a true relationship for a few faults. Nobody is perfect and at the end affection is always greater than perfection.' Ritu Ghatourey

Affection is the language of love that gets more fluent the more you speak it, more expressive the more you express it and more loving the more you love it and enjoy it. Most people feel affectionate towards their partners – but it is in showing it that we keep love vibrant and rich and it is only by showing it that we get familiar with it and content in it. As ever, it's a matter of practising it.

Feeling and showing affection make you all the more fond of each other, and caring and loving. It has a wonderful effect in every way.

It is, for instance, one of the greatest ingredients in making love not just willingly but eagerly. It lets passion back in, spices your senses and adds an ecstatic edge to your sensuality, and in so doing it becomes a fantastic aphrodisiac, reminding us that actually sex feels amazing and would be a great idea.

Having said that, it's good to remember that affection is autonomous – it stands alone as a bright aspect of your relationship in its own right and it's important not to assume it will lead to lovemaking. Without expectations of sex you're free to enjoy it for its own sake with no hidden or overt sexual agenda or demands.

Being affectionate and receiving your partner's affection gladly also reminds you that you love each other. Do and should you need reminding? Probably! For it's so easy to forget it in the hustle and bustle of life and to shrug each other's attentions off with an 'I'm really busy' or 'I'm tired' or 'I don't feel like it'. Affection gives and receives a hug anyway, and if you relax and enjoy it, it reminds you that there's nothing more important than giving each other your time, raising your energy to enjoy each other's presence and closeness, and turning any apathy about your togetherness back into enthusiasm. There are few things so good as loving and being loved. In showing and accepting affection you hold love in your heart and hands. It is very, very precious in your relationship. Treasure it.

ENJOY THE EXPERIENCE OF TOUCH FEARLESSLY

Practise being tactile – every day. What's not to like about being affectionately tactile? Surprisingly, often the reason one or both partners shy away from physical affection is a fear that it will lead to sex. So a key to relaxing into it is to know that it isn't about sex. This can be amazingly liberating, allowing you to bring affection back into your relationship in a blissfully pleasurable way for both of you. So agree with your partner that neither of you will assume that affection will necessarily lead to sex. Then you can both relax completely, free to enjoy affection for its own sake, which is very precious in its own right. There are few things in life as wonderful as tactile affection – it just feels amazing to be close, to snuggle up to each other, caress and be caressed. Once you know neither of you is expecting to have sex just because you're enjoying closeness, it enables you to choose to at the right time for both of you. It's a kind of reverse psychology that makes physical affection indirectly a brilliant aphrodisiac

MAKE A HABIT OF BEING AFFECTIONATE

Practise feeling affectionate. Can you choose to feel affectionate – isn't it a spontaneous thing whether you do or don't? Yes of course it can be spontaneous and that's lovely. But you can also choose to feel affectionate. You know the feeling and can bring it into being at will whenever you remember it and relive it in the moment. And the great thing about this practice is that like most skills and habits the more you do it the more likely it is to be spontaneous. Be aware, if at first you find it difficult to feel and think affectionately of each other, that it may be because you didn't learn to be from your parents' example when you were children, or you've since somehow been put off it. It's never too late to learn, or if you've just got out of the habit of feeling affectionate towards your nearest and dearest, to bring it back into the dynamic between you. It's about feeling fond of each other and wanting to express that in a positive way. Start to think of how you can do this more and more. In all kinds of daily situations you can focus on feeling this affection. For instance, when doing your food shop in the supermarket, think affectionately of your partner and enjoy the thought of pleasing them with the meals you'll make and enjoy together.

SHOW YOUR PLEASURE IN EACH OTHER'S AFFECTION

Reward each other whenever you are affectionate. It feels so good when your partner expresses pleasure at something you've done for them and it encourages you to repeat it often and look for other ways of getting a similarly pleased reaction. Think of it like purring. When a cat's stroked affectionately it automatically purrs with pleasure and it feels like a generous thank you. This pleased response resonates with your body and mind and makes you feel good too. It's surprisingly deeply relaxing and has also been found to trigger a healing response. It's even more so when a couple act affectionately with each other. It's therapeutic in drawing you close, physically and emotionally, and as long as it's never demanded, it may awaken sexual desire too. Either way, it's magically sensuous and makes you glow with pleasure and love. So make a point of never shying away from an affectionate gesture whether words, touch or a loving look. Respond generously and affection between you will grow and thrive, making your relationship a loving, wonderful place to be.

Putting it all together

Affection is like an emotional and physical lubricant! It frees up your motivation to feel loving to each other and to express that love in all kinds of affectionate ways. The more affectionate you are to each other, the easier it becomes until it's a habit – a natural way of being around each other. Realize that affectionate touch is one of the great pleasures of being a couple but don't confuse it with necessarily being a prelude to sex. Remember always that the Secret of it being an aphrodisiac is not to expect it to be… or to demand of your partner that being tactile will lead to foreplay or even sexual intercourse. Treat affection as a pleasure in its own right without anticipating sex. Then you are both free to enjoy your closeness and the pleasure of touch to the full. It is an aphrodisiac – but a slow acting one, since you realize there is no demand or expectation today and it's only to be taken advantage of when and if you are both ready.

Quite simply, affection is one of the greatest pleasures of togetherness and life.

8) Be loyal

9
10
11
12
13
14
15
16
17
18
19
20
21
22
23
24
25
26
27
28
29
30
31
32
33
34
35
36
37
38
39
40
41
42
43
44
45
46
47
48
49
50

❝ *'Love is friendship that has caught fire. It is loyalty through good and bad times. It settles for less than perfection and makes allowances for human weaknesses.'* Ann Landers

❝ *'I love loyalty. I love trust.'* Elton John

❝ *'For above all things Love means sweetness, and truth, and measure; yea, loyalty to the loved one and to your word.'*
Marie de France

❝ *'Loyalty evokes in us the knowledge that they are faithful to us and would never betray us by their behaviour or in their speech.'* Rosy Anderson

❝ *'Most important in a friendship? Tolerance and loyalty.'*
J. K. Rowling

Knowing that your partner is there for you – loyal and trustworthy and 100 per cent for you – is one of the greatest gifts in a relationship and indeed in the whole world. It's something you give to each other on a constant, unimpeachable basis, and it creates and keeps current a strong, unquestioning bond of confidence in each other.

Like all the Secrets it's based on a decision followed by attention. Even when your love is sure and mutually valued, it's very possible to forget to back each other up, or to think it funny or clever to disrespect each other. However amusing though, it undermines your respect for them in time and can cause hurt, since pretty

31

soon you won't be doing it when you're alone with your friends, but when you're both in company. Disloyalty will unsettle your friends anyway for they of course will realize that if you aren't true to your partner, you certainly won't be true to them.

Loyalty doesn't come in half-measures. You are either loyal or you're not and if you're not, your partner will feel betrayed and their love for you will be dented. In time these dents intrude into the fabric of the love you share.

True, trustworthy loyalty on the other hand creates a warm glow between you. It provides a solid foundation for your love and your whole relationship.

It also feels good to be loyal. You'll respect yourself more as well as your partner. And when you're loyal your partner will of course know it and it will take only a little thought and determination to return the compliment and be loyal to you too.

It's also one of the greatest factors for happiness in family life. Children love their parents to be united. They may try to play you off against each other, but if you don't back each other up they will deep down be disappointed. They want you to be in agreement with each other – however much they try to push the boundaries you set for them, they will actually love the fact that they know you are a mutual support system because then they will feel safe and have confidence in you and your decisions.

It's a hugely important Secret of happiness in your relationship and a deep love between you that lasts, strong and sure, no matter what's going on in your lives.

AVOID CRITICIZING YOUR PARTNER TO OTHERS

When you're with friends without your partner, don't be tempted to start criticizing him. If your friends are being disparaging about their partners, you can listen quietly or steer them away from negativity. If there's a problem, suggest they talk it over with their partners and find a positive and constructive way forward. If they've just got into a negative groove of thought, say 'Hey – let's not be so negative' or 'You know what, we choose to be with them – let's think of all their good points – there are lots of them'. In other words, encourage them to be loyal – as well as helping them it will make it easier for you to be loyal too. Ensure that you don't follow suit by criticizing your partner. If there's an issue you need help with, best of all talk to your partner calmly and lovingly. If they won't meet you halfway like this, see a counsellor who will be objective and can expertly help you deal with the issue and will keep it completely confidential – don't betray your partner by discussing them with friends who may tell others.

BE ON THE SAME TEAM

In company together, remember you're on the same side – a couple, together because you love each other. This doesn't mean, of course, that you'll always agree about everything. But it does mean that you'll defend to the hilt your right to think individually and independently of each other and won't ever challenge or sabotage this right. So be nice to and about each other and each other's opinions when you're in company. It is fine to say you disagree if you're asked, but don't make a big thing of it. Never be nasty and never belittle them. Always show your respect and love in your words and body language. Let everyone know you're a team and hot on mutual support. It's comforting and inspiring to relax in the knowledge that your partner is there for you and values you and what you say, even if they don't necessarily agree with you. It's comfortable for those around you too; the only thing worse than hearing someone criticize their partner in public is hearing them both do it!

It's important to be aware it's not funny. Pretending it is still shows aggression, veiled in the pretence it's 'just teasing'. Refuse to attack each other or backbite; supporting each other in public will do your relationship the world of good.

SHOW A UNITED FRONT TO OTHERS

When you're with your children and other family members, practise presenting a united, loving front. Although your kids may try to play you against each other, they will appreciate it if you back each other up, whereas it will only unsettle them and give them dangerously mixed messages if you don't. So whenever possible, without compromising your integrity, back each other up. Where you really feel you can't, discuss it with each other and reach a decision you can both honour before you go back to the children. Discuss the importance of this kind of mutual loyalty with your partner so that you are sure to both support each other this way. Remember that kids like you to be united – it makes them feel safe and happy that you are leaders who agree with each other. They want you to agree! So be strong in agreement. It's important, too, to show loyalty to each other when you're apart and when you're together. Criticizing each other will make not just the pair of you unhappy but also your children, so praise each other as much as possible and encourage each other to be good partners, good parents, good people and, above all, loyal.

Putting it all together

Appreciate how good it feels to be loyal and trustworthy to and about each other and notice how relaxed this makes you both and how much more others relax around you too.

Loyalty is natural when we are first in love but can gradually erode if life pressures overtake you. Don't let them create a wedge between you – be aware of how important mutual trust and loyalty are and keep them firmly central to your relationship.

One of the great pluses of being in a committed relationship is the feeling of being a team. You're on the same side, rooting for each other and cheering each other on. As a team of two, it's very important not to let each other down by going offside; you only have each other in this union – you need to be there for each other, always, and to know you can put your faith in each other.

And it's one of the greatest feelings on this Earth to know that you have a partner who is always there for you, loving you and wanting only the best for you, ready with their support, steadfastly and reliably faithful.

Enjoy being loyal to each other and, if you have children, enjoy knowing you are setting them a great example of trust and loyalty.

It will have a big impact on your mutual happiness and keep your love as strong and true as the support and trust you share.

9 Be sensitive, intuitive and perceptive

> 'We can be blind to the obvious, and blind to our blindness.'
> Daniel Kahneman

> 'We have basic psychological needs. Love recognizes all these needs. If any are unmet, the individual can never be totally realized.' Leo Buscaglia

> 'Love is sensitivity, love is consciousness… The heart in love remains soft and sensitive.' Anthony de Mello

> 'Manners are a sensitive awareness of the feelings of others. If you have that awareness, you have good manners, no matter what fork you use.' Emily Post

> 'Romantic love is a passionate spiritual-emotional-sexual attachment that reflects a high regard for the value of each other's person.' Nathaniel Branden

Early on we're tuned in to each other. We notice everything about our partner and about the way we're getting on. It fascinates, compels and thrills us. And it helps our love develop and deepen. You did this with your partner – got to know each other really, really well. And you loved being alert to each other, knowing, seeing.

But the minutiae and complexity and busyness of life gradually returns and takes over the exclusivity of the relationship. Also, paradoxically, because you've got to know each other so well you may stop the learning curve and, without realizing it, cease to know each other very well because you're always changing, always growing, and if you don't keep up with what's going on with each other, suddenly you can become like strangers without realizing it.

So it's hugely important to stay aware. To observe each other with all your senses. To see yourself too and the impact – or lack of impact – that you are having on your partner and they on you.

Some questions to ask yourself now, and every now and then as the years go by, are: 'How are you getting on?' Really getting on, that is? 'Have you thought of it lately – reviewed your relationship?' 'Have you noticed how much you're noticing them, looking at them lovingly, seeing the real them?'

It's so good to do it because it's so easy to neglect each other. I'm not only talking about thoughtfulness of small daily creature-comforts like cooking food you know your partner loves, or doing necessary maintenance work on their car. Important though these kindnesses and courtesies are what this Secret is even more about is staying in tune with the inner wellbeing of each other's spirit.

In the beginning we look at each other with love. We see each other not just externally but the true essence of our being. In seeing – noticing with all your senses – you fell in love with each other and your great awareness of each other nurtured your rapport and kept you singing together with joy.

For ongoing happiness and indeed much bliss together, keep looking at each other, really seeing, really noticing, and feel the love flow between you, always.

PAY ATTENTION TO EACH OTHER

Recognize the need to notice each other. Ask yourself if you're paying attention to your partner, and really noticing and taking in how they are. You can sleep together, get up in the morning, have breakfast, meet again later and, unbelievably but it very easily happens, not really take in each other's wellbeing – or 'ill being' – at all. Remember that you're on automatic pilot much of the time – we all are – but be careful that it's not all the time. Make absolutely sure that you focus on your partner now and then and they on you. Check out their state of health, for instance, how well they're eating and other physical signs of feeling good, and as or even more importantly, how they are feeling, what kind of mood they're in, whether they are happy in their work, how fulfilled they are in other ways, how well the two of you are relating, whether you're making love and enjoying it? Sounds like an awful lot of questions and it is; and they are all hugely relevant to your individual and your relationship's happiness. But don't be alarmed – the questions only take a few moments and will become second nature after you've practised running through them a few times. It's about sharpening your perceptive skills and all it takes is a small amount of intent, time and love.

APPRECIATE YOUR PARTNER AND EXPECT THEIR APPRECIATION

Appreciate your partner and expect and encourage them to appreciate you. It's good to talk about the need as, un-voiced, it can go unrecognized and eventually be completely forgotten. More relationships die of neglect than bad behaviour. People all too often stop noticing each other's inner being. A client whose partner recently announced she wanted a divorce and left him, said he was shocked as he'd had no idea she was unhappy. 'She was there, every day, same as usual,' he told me and asked 'I would have known if she'd been unhappy, wouldn't I?' Well no, actually, he wouldn't and clearly didn't because, as he began to realize, he'd taken her for granted and stopped any kind of meaningful communication with her. He'd had no idea how she really was for months and perhaps even years. Nor did he have any insight into how he was himself. There was no active, noticed and nurtured happiness in their relationship – just neglect and even that wasn't intentional or noticed. If only they'd realized in time.

Don't let this happen to you. Notice your partner with loving consideration and care and let them know you are highly aware of them and alert to the way they are and want to do all you can to promote their wellbeing. Ask them to look out for you, too. The great thing about it is that it feels wonderful.

PUT LOVE AND ENERGY INTO YOUR ATTENTIVE INTERACTION

Like all aspects of your relationship, the two of you both contribute to the dynamic between you and benefit hugely when the input is willing and enthusiastic.

So don't hide your interest in your partner: let your partner know you love them to bits and, because you love them, notice how they are, take an interest and want to do all you can to be there for them and encourage their true happiness and health, mind, body and spirit. Tell them how much you appreciate them seeing you in your own entirety and complexity too. Then you can relate in the best way possible – knowingly and sensitively lovingly. Use any and all of the other Secrets to help you – they work together, each one a catalyst sparking a vibrant energy between you and, together, enabling your love to last and grow richer, ever developing through the various phases and stages of life.

Putting it all together

There's the saddest song by Tom Waits: 'You haven't looked at me that way in years. But I'm still here.' Don't let that happen to the two of you, with either or both scarcely noticing who and how you each are these days.

For if you don't see or otherwise notice your partner – really attentively look and pay attention to them – how can you know how they are, not just physically but mentally and emotionally too?

And if you don't notice them, it's only another step or two down the same route to not caring. Or perhaps the not caring comes first?

Instead, take great care to remember how much you do care about each other. Be very sensitive to each other and look at each other through eyes of love. As you consciously remember to give your love with your eyes and other gestures, you will feel it flooding through you.

Remember how strongly you loved each other when you first met and what you were both like then and think how you've each changed and grown, matured and developed. Be aware of each other's new interests as well as enduring ones and think of what you love about your lives and life together and, as well, what you perhaps don't like, for no one is perfect. Notice it all and take it in. Be glad you are both who you are now and that you are still together, still loving each other. Look at each other with eyes of love. I shamelessly repeat it – I can't repeat it enough. It is one, if not the most vital, of the secrets of lasting love.

Look at each other – and see and sense each other – with eyes of love.

$\bigl(|0\bigr)$ Cope well with conflict

❝ *'Change and growth take place when a person has risked himself and dares to become involved with experimenting with his own life.'* Herbert A. Otto

❝ *'Real love always creates, it never destroys.'* Leo Buscaglia

❝ *'All war is a symptom of man's failure as a thinking animal.'* John Steinbeck

❝ *'Peace is not the absence of conflict but the presence of creative alternatives for responding to conflict – alternatives to passive or aggressive responses, alternatives to violence.'* Dorothy Thompson

❝ *'Ideas and not battles mark the forward progress of mankind.'* L. Ron Hubbard

The key to coping with conflict is thought. Before lashing out or seething in painful silence when negative emotions rear up between you, remember this: although a couple, you are still two people, individuals with often differing ideas and ways of doing things.

When you first got to know each other, you were delighted to discover all the many things you have in common and you found you were so amazingly compatible you could easily, you hoped, live together in harmony. You probably didn't foresee much conflict, if any. But, after the honeymoon months or years, like most couples you will have lost that in-love habit of slotting easily into agreement. You remembered you both have strong wills of your own and wanted to have your will again, most or at least a good part of the time.

So some conflict is natural. The Secret of its peaceful presence in a happy relationship – your happy relationship – is about dealing positively and constructively with the conflict between you when the natural wish of each of you for individual autonomy clashes.

The first step is recognizing it and not feeling guilty about it or about the plethora of emotions that have suddenly engulfed you. They are natural, too, in your insistence on being your natural selves – individuals.

Once you register this – and doing so is a habit you can choose to adopt and it only takes a nanosecond – you are in the strong, centred position of knowing what's going on. Now you'll find you can shake off the negative feelings undermining your serenity and move forwards in clarity to use your common sense, love and all-round intelligence to find the best way to deal with the dispute.

It could be a matter of finding a resolution that suits you both or deciding on the best decision to go with in the circumstances. Talking it through may well find one or both of you changing your opinion and seeing there is perhaps another better way. So willingness to listen to each other as you state your case calmly and without rancour is key. As is a willingness to let go of pre-held conceptions when they are not apt or beneficial to this particular situation.

And always remember: willingness to accept each other's right to their views and to take turns at decision-making is vital too.

BE AWARE OF CONFLICT

Register conflict the minute it arises. It's surprisingly easy to pretend it isn't happening, whether it's you or your partner who is out of sorts. But it's best to be fully alert to it and address it. You'll know the feeling; it might be an insidious feeling of being thwarted that creeps up on you, or a sudden flash of anger that comes out of the ether. But suddenly you'll be aware of feeling negative, whether narky, cross or outraged at being crossed. Take a moment to consider the word 'cross' because it's very apt – being crossed causes anger. Just recognizing when it happens and why goes a long way to defusing the surge of negativity and regaining your inner calm. The Secret is to pay attention to the negative feeling before it streams out of you through your body or verbal language. For anger vented blindly never helps, always hurts and will cause fear and very probably reactive anger in your partner.

Once in control of your frustration or fury you can regain your calm. Once unruffled and composed you'll find you can address the cause of the stress or conflict rationally, logically and constructively. But you may not need to as you might well find it has already settled or disappeared.

TREAT CONFLICT CONSTRUCTIVELY

Think constructively about what you can do to lessen the differences between you. Review the circumstances – think of it as making a calm, objective recce.

Consider what you want from your partner and what they want from you in this situation, listening to each other's ideas and wishes. Remember you are both perfectly entitled to your own views, even if they have changed from earlier ones you were familiar with. Deal with the conflict where you are now, refusing to drag up slurs and slights from the past and being especially careful not to slag each other off using past incidents as fuel. Raking up what you've said or done in the past will only fuel today's anger and skew the present situation. Concentrate on the situation in hand and how you can constructively address it. Let common sense reign for both of you, helping you review options and make a logical, unbiased decision about the best thing to do in the circumstances. Remember though that your partner's logic may differ from yours! Mutual respect helps greatly and maintaining a sense of humour can work wonders in helping you work together. Refuse to be huffy or touchy about this.

BRING LOVE INTO THE EQUATION

It's easy, when you're each trying to get your own way, to forget that this is the person you love so much that you choose to live with them and share yourselves and your life. Remembering you love each other will likely be a difficult concept in the moment but a wry smile will make you feel worlds better. Love, respect and kindness really are all you need. Ask yourselves: 'What's the loving way forward here?' Of course you are both important – your views, needs and wishes. But you love each other, so find a way to accommodate each other's views.

As in most of the Secrets, this one is largely about balance, so think in terms of weighing the options, your wishes, the boundaries and aspects of the circumstances.

Love is in the detail as much as your attitudes. With love in the equation, any dispute can be settled or, somehow and sometimes, is best simply laid to rest with you agreeing to differ.

Putting it all together

Your partnership is made up of two individuals – you and your partner – two distinct, autonomous lives sharing, voluntarily and in a spirit of love, one life. It's a mutual choice you continue to make every single day. You are free to make this choice – and as you are together because you want to be, your relationship is very much a democracy. You're bound to annoy each other sometimes, to rub each other up the wrong way, to want to do some things in different ways, to clash over decisions to be made. You're bound to sometimes yearn for your old, pre-relationship freedom to make your own decisions. But you are together – your mutual choice – so be glad. And be glad to negotiate solutions, resolve disputes and keep your separate selves running in tandem, not on the exact track but on parallel tracks. Use logic, fairness, trust, intelligence (including emotional intelligence), understanding, all your senses and above and around all, love, to find the best way forward for the two of you and others involved. You are a team. Play together, lovingly.

Make time to be together

66 *'Take time to love and be loved – it is the privilege of the gods.'*
Old English proverb

66 *'You will never find time for anything. If you want time, you must make it.'* Charles Buxton

66 *'Don't wait. The time will never be just right.'* Napoleon Hill

66 *'Time is the most valuable thing a man can spend.'*
Diogenes Laërtius

66 *'Set priorities for your goals. A major part of successful living lies in the ability to put first things first. Indeed, the reason most major goals are not achieved is that we spend our time doing second things first.'* Robert J. McKain

You want a happy relationship. It is one of the top (if not the paramount) priorities for you and your partner. Love – and thus a happy relationship – needs attention and can only flourish and feel good if we give it time generously and lovingly. But top priorities get pushed down the list of things to do if we don't prioritize them. It sounds obvious and yet, as you've probably found, it's so easy to get caught up in all the other daily chores and then you find yet another day has passed where you've neglected each other. If neglected, love withers. Cherished with attention, love keeps blossoming throughout a lifetime together.

But how, you may be protesting, can we find time when we're so busy? As in the wise quote above, if we expect to magically find time, we're unlikely to. The truth is, it is up to you and your partner to make time to be together, to pay attention to each other, to do things together, to make love, to be affectionate, to laugh together, to share, in other words, your lives and your love for each other. It's about generosity and giving. Not just giving of your time to do things for each other, but generously receiving each other's attention. It doesn't mean you have to actively be doing something together all the time you're together. Often just being in each other's presence can be loving and quietly contenting as you bask in the moments you're gently sharing. But it is important to now and then focus on each other, talk with each other, taking care to share your thoughts and listen intelligently and with your heart engaged too.

It's about gladness. And being glad to have each other's commitment to being together – that you made and continue to make the choice to be with each other. And being delighted, on an ongoing basis, in each other's company. It's about feeling the joy of your love and showing it. Making and taking time for each other is the greatest gift you can give each other. It's the lifeblood of the happiness in your relationship.

MAKE YOUR TOGETHERNESS A PRIORITY

A host of other things are waiting in the wings ready to pounce on your time and devour it, so be vigilant. Remember every day why you're together: because you love each other and want to be happy together, and make time with each other your top priority. No excuses: if you get in the habit of filling your day with events and time spent, however nobly meant, with others, it will soon become habitual and day after day will go by when you and your partner drift a little further apart. Long tracts of time together every day aren't essential, and there may be an exceptional day now and then when you see little of each other, but most days prioritize at least some quality time together. This means paying loving, interested attention to each other's thoughts and wellbeing and enjoying each other's company. On some days plan to share longer interludes where you can hold hands literally and metaphorically. It may sound a bit mechanical to prioritize togetherness, but it honestly is the only way if you both lead busy lives. And it will soon become a lovely way of being where your mutual attention to and wish for togetherness is automatic.

SYNCHRONIZE YOUR SCHEDULES

With different work, hobby and parenting schedules and different body clocks, you need to synchronize times when you're both able to spend time together and will have the energy to focus on each other enthusiastically. Over and over in counselling I hear one partner say 'I'm too tired to interact with her in the evening' or 'I don't feel like making love when I wake up'. Stop focusing on the negatives and agree, positively, on times when you both feel good and are prepared to give each other that most valuable gift of all — your time.

Over and over again I hear similar refrains: 'I don't have time to sit down and cuddle (or talk, or make love, or go for a walk, etc.)' As I said above and I will stress it over and over again, ensure you make time. We are given 24 hours in every day to use as we please and plan. Sure, 7 or 8 hours is set aside for sleeping, and work and childcare takes another significant tract, but other than that the day is yours to choose to enjoy some time together as a couple. That's what your relationship is all about — it's not merely a framework around which you hang all elements of your lives — it's your chosen decision to relate happily to each other. Make time! It's about love and happiness. What's not to like?

IMPROVE THE QUALITY OF YOUR TIME TOGETHER

Being together if you're detached and thinking of other things and people isn't the same as being together in a connected and interactive way. Detachment feels cold and signals you'd rather not be together. It doesn't feel good for either of you. So put your heart and energy into a willingness to connect. It shows a lively interest in each other and a real wish and ability to enjoy your togetherness. It's vital to your happiness, individually and as a couple, to take a real interest in each other. It shows you care about what's going on in your lives and how you both are.

Remember, too, that the whole point of getting together with your partner was to enhance each other's life. It still is – why would you want to stay together if you didn't? So be aware of the impact you're having on your partner, and they on you, and make a point of checking that you are doing just that – improving or enriching each other's wellbeing in some way. Have fun together. Actively enjoy each other's company. Be affectionate, tactile. Be in love with each other. Suddenly when you think of a connection like this it becomes meaningful and appealing to be nice to each other. Spending time together and connecting – really connecting – is meaningful and appealing and nice! Light up your partner's life and you'll light up your own. It's the opposite of neglect and it feels wonderful.

Putting it all together

It's so easy to spend time together and be nice to each other and it's the main purpose of a relationship. I don't mean sickly sweet or falsely. I mean interested, loving and fully engaged and interacting with each other. It makes a huge difference to your individual happiness and the whole wellbeing of your relationship. It's very easy to forget this in the hustle and bustle, challenges and demands of everyday life though; it takes a conscious decision and a certain amount of effort to initiate rescheduling your diaries to fit each other in. It may seem strange initially to prioritize an hour, say, together in the evening doing something together, instead of devoting all your time to the television or the Internet. So remember that your relationship is actually what's most important. It's a living, ever-changing thing and it needs your active, energetic, willing and above all enthusiastic input. Be glad, every day, that you are with this person who you love and who loves you. Give thanks to your God or the universe or yourself for the gift you share of love and chosen togetherness. And decide – both of you – to care for your relationship lovingly and positively. Every day. It matters. Make sure you matter to each other – and show it every day with your loving, freely given time.

12 Balance work, home and play

'Work is love made visible.' Kahlil Gibran

'One can live magnificently in this world if one knows how to work and how to love.' Leo Tolstoy

'Love and work are the cornerstones of our humanness.' Sigmund Freud

'Being the richest man in the cemetery doesn't matter to me. Going to bed at night saying we've done something wonderful… that's what matters to me.' Steve Jobs

'If I'd known she would leave, and how much I would miss her, I wouldn't have spent so much time at work.' Self-confessed recovering workaholic – Anon

Just as we need to love, we need to work. We were born to love and be loved. It's there the minute we are born and probably beforehand. Our capacity for love is in everything we do and our whole experience of life as well as, of course, our prime relationships. The wish to work and the ability to enjoy it, full on, is also intrinsic. Both are developed by our upbringing and, with good teachers and role models, help us flourish – at loving and at working. They both impact hugely on our personal and relationship happiness and fulfilment and they work together or in juxtaposition. There is a learnable art to balancing them and where there is the potential for art, there is the energy of creativity. It feels good and is immensely satisfying, however challenging it may be!

49

Balance is vital, since if one or both of you devote too much time to your careers, your relationship will be denuded of time together and enough personal inter-attention. On the other hand, if one of you doesn't have any personal work satisfaction, the frustration, however well hidden, may seep into your relationship. This doesn't mean you both have to have careers. Work is the productive use of your time in a way that's meaningful and fulfilling for you, personally. It's about living as fully and enthusiastically as you possibly can in all kinds of ways: it could be bringing up children, going out to work, working from home, voluntary work, pursuing your chosen art or craft skills, which fully engages you – any commitment to living fulfillingly and enthusiastically all count. If you are happy in your work it will reflect in the happiness of your relationship.

But don't let work take you over. Remember how valuable your relationship is to both of you and cherish your 'couple time'. Be ready to let go of your work during your time together. Your relationship also depends on your mutual commitment to loving and engaging with each other fulfillingly and enthusiastically. Is it hard work? Absolutely not: fulfilment and enthusiasm lift work and togetherness to a level of enjoyment and deep satisfaction. Enjoy!

CREATE A GOOD WORK/LIFE BALANCE

Stay aware of the balance between work and your life together and keep it in tune. Keeping your relationship running sweetly through the years takes commitment, a little energy, the wish to keep loving each other and get on well. It takes attention. Maintaining your enjoyment of work has much the same requirements. If one or other places excessive demands on your time and energy on a daily basis, it throws the fine balance between them out of kilter. Working too hard under pressure can do it, so can working long hours every day. Demanding too much time and engagement for your love life can also cause difficulty. Manage your working hours effectively and fairly and if anxiety about your work is running into your leisure hours, have a clear appraisal to see what can be done to ease the pressure. Learning relaxation techniques can also be helpful in leaving work where it belongs, in the workplace, and not seeping into your relationship. Similarly, don't let your togetherness, or wish for more of it, intrude into your working hours. At work be professional. At home be loving. That way the two complement each other and enrich your lives together too.

SHARE ROUTINE JOBS AND RESPONSIBILITIES FAIRLY

Running the life you share together involves a lot of maintenance – hard work if done under duress or shouldered alone, fulfilling, enjoyable work if willingly done and fairly shared. We all enjoy different things in different ways, so every now and then sit down together to go through who does which chores and looks after other aspects of your home, family and couple life. It's amazing how many people are regularly doing a chore they hate doing when a little bit of communication would result in their partner taking it over or at least their turn. Have a family plan for daily chores too. Once they get used to it, kids enjoy being involved and it's good for them. And if you're both in paid work, agreeing to pay for some outside help often makes good financial and relationship sense. Contribute fairly to your leisure and social life too. Give and take. Be generous, be fair and never, ever be a martyr.

HELP EACH OTHER FIND FULFILMENT AND SATISFACTION

It's really easy to be self-centred about work but in a relationship it's important and feels good to take lots of interest in each other's work. It isn't about the content of the work so much and the fine details, but rather the emotional place your partner's currently in, the inspiration they're finding and the overall fulfilment. We promote each other's wellbeing by encouraging the finding of our right individual paths of work – work ideally that moves us and fills us with gladness and enthusiasm but at least provides us with the contentment and satisfaction of work willingly undertaken. It isn't about riches and celebrity – the kind of 'success' that many desire so much. True success is being pleased to have the work we do have, whatever it is. There is a simple but great pleasure in time spent productively and helpfully to others in some way, and there is another bonus of satisfaction that comes at the end of a task well done, a day's work finished. Help each other to realize and enjoy these treasures and be glad – and satisfied – together.

Putting it all together

Sharing the pleasure we get from our work and our attitudes and feelings about it feels good and encourages the flow of love. It's about being interested in each other – a way of showing and growing your love and mutual understanding. A rich love life will increase your tendency to want to work and inspire you to work well. So the fulfilment and satisfaction of working willingly and loving actively mix together in an alchemy of pleasure, ongoing development and lasting enjoyment. Life is far too short to waste in working at things we begrudge doing or to stay in a relationship we begrudge being in. 'Begrudgement' tends to seep into and sour the rest of our life too. So it makes sense to make a positive choice to enjoy whatever it is we are working at, and if that isn't the work choice we want for ever, to use it as a useful raft from which to explore what alternative work we could do that we would enjoy more.

And it makes sense to choose to love each other enthusiastically and to share yourselves with each other generously in so many wonderful ways as the Secrets show. Fulfilling, enjoyable love and work are there for your choosing. Pay attention to them – and make it loving, encouraging, joyous attention. They are blessings you give to yourselves and each other. Treasure them – for they give you heaven on earth.

13 Assume nothing – seek only truth

> 'Living with integrity means: Not settling for less than what you know you deserve in your relationships. Asking for what you want and need from others. Speaking your truth, even though it might create conflict or tension. Behaving in ways that are in harmony with your personal values. Making choices based on what you believe, and not what others believe.' Barbara De Angelis

> 'Anyone who doesn't take truth seriously in small matters cannot be trusted in large ones either.' Albert Einstein

> 'There are only two mistakes one can make along the road to truth; not going all the way, and not starting.' Buddha

> 'If you look for truth, you may find comfort in the end; if you look for comfort you will not get either comfort or truth only soft soap and wishful thinking.' C. S. Lewis

> 'Truth is a deep kindness that teaches us to be content in our everyday life and share with the people the same happiness.'
> Khalil Gibran

This Secret applies as much to life generally as, even more crucially, relationships. In life and love we've a tendency to fly along held up by assumptions. They range from pretty good norms, conventions and traditions forged from common sense and experience to spurious expectations, hopes, misplaced trust and wild wishes. If one assumption to which we've misguidedly latched a lot of our belief system happens to be punctured, there we are – falling through the air shocked and bewildered.

Apart from the obvious danger of getting hurt, you stand to miss out on the reality of the situation, which could be far better and more enjoyable than you realize, and you can also miss the opportunity for real learning about each other and the dynamics between you, and thus developing your relationship.

Truth is what is. No point pretending otherwise or not bothering to clarify it as if we do that we're living with and probably under an illusion.

You might, for example, assume your partner feels the same as you about some aspect of your life together, denying them their truth. Or you might consciously pretend to be something you're not, or to feel something you don't, letting him live in the bubble of illusion, deluded and set up for, at some stage, disappointment.

Truth is real. It lets you get to grips with anything that's wrong and appreciate to the full what's very much right. It frees you of 'glamours' – the unspoken words and feelings and confusions that hang in the air around us. When we face up to the truth and 'fess up, we give ourselves a brilliant chance of changing what needs to be changed and deciding not to waste time dithering around what might be, but isn't. Best of all, it feels so much better to know exactly where we are. Then we can listen to each other speaking honestly, we can hear each other clearly, we can have a dialogue that's deeply interesting and lets us in on each other's truth and the real way we're relating.

It's easy to get swept along by our assumptions and live in a landscape that isn't really there. Don't assume. Check out, look, see – really see each other (as in Secret 9). A misperception, however tempting to believe, will only let you down – and probably already has. Face up to the truth and hard though it may be at first, it will be your friend. Truth is your true friend – and your partner's – and your relationship's.

KNOW YOURSELF

Knowing who you are sounds so obvious and yet it's a curious mixture of the simple and the complex. We complicate self-knowledge by any pretence we make to ourselves and others.

With yourself, for instance, you might pretend you are better at something than you actually are. 'I'm a very loving person,' one client assured me, believing it until we'd explored what love meant and how they were, or actually weren't, behaving lovingly at all. Or, even more likely, you may be denigrating yourself and your abilities. Then you can do it with your partner – making out to them that you are better or worse in some way than you are. If they do the same, both of you end up living in a world of make believe.

Far better to take time to review who you are at this time of your life, what matters to you, which path you want to be on. Don't put yourself or your partner down. Be the best 'you' that you each can and want to be. Encourage your partner to do the same. Listen to your inner voices and your hearts and to each other. Really listen. It's part of love and happiness and living well in this amazing world – and living well within your relationship.

Listen to your truth and live your truth honestly and it will transform the way you are and the way you relate to each other. It doesn't, of course, mean you're approving bad habits, etc. – it simply means you are justifiably feeling good about your good points and blessings. It also means you are recognizing any not-so-good things that can do with changing and starting to make improvements.

EMBRACE TRUTH

Being aware of your truth and the truth of your relationship is good – the next step is to live in it by continuing to behave truthfully and positively. It's wonderful to say 'I love you' but the truth of it is in the doing. As you live out your love in all kinds of small ways – for instance, small acts of kindness, gestures and a loving, appreciative attitude to each other – your love will thrive and develop as you both develop, the way you are meant to be, and each encouraging and being glad for the other's wellbeing and progress through life. This way you can adjust to your individual ups and downs, always keeping in step in your relationship. Mutual support is one of the most precious gifts of a relationship. Give it generously, from your heart.

PRACTISE BEING TRUTHFUL

Being truthful needs you to practise it on an ongoing basis. Watch you don't fall into a pattern of pleasing yourself and your partner at the expense of reality. Most of us are so schooled to be polite, to hide our feelings and to shy away from helping others to speak up, that our best intentions of living and loving truthfully with our partner can slide if we're not watchful. If I catch myself in pleasing mode (the one I was brought up to adopt as my default setting!) I find it helps to pause every now and then and ask myself: 'What's going on here, Jenny? Are you being genuinely congruent? Is this really true?' You'll know if not because you'll feel kind of embarrassed and resistant. But recognize the truth and embrace it and your heart will sing instead. And if you detect dishonesty in the ether, try to remember to home in on it and see what the cause is. There's always a cause. Be courageous in finding and admitting it.

Putting it all together

It takes courage to face the truth, to see hidden agendas, to risk enabling change. You may feel it will encourage you and your partner to be selfish but it's the opposite. We respect each other when we are truthful and we show our self-respect. It enables the best way of living and loving together. It enables development as against stagnation. It doesn't mean you stop trying to be the best, kindest most loving and lovable people you are, in fact the opposite – it encourages and enables you to be all those things genuinely, congruently and consistently because it's real, not a sham. You may sense, sometimes, that tact and sensitivity are called for when your partner is emotionally fragile, but that's not the same as a habit of pretence. When truth is your way of being, everything will fall into place. And, because you and your partner are being your true, best selves, you will be free to love – in truth and trust.

14 Be generous

❝ *'Generosity is giving more than you can.'* Khalil Gibran

❝ *'Make space in your life for the things that matter, for family and friends, love and generosity, fun and joy.'* Jonathan Sacks

❝ *'Meanness has no place in a relationship – it stifles it. Generosity of spirit draws you together, opens your hearts and creates a buzz of joy.'* Rosie Hallett

❝ *'If instead of a gem, or even a flower, we should cast the gift of a loving thought into the heart of a friend, that would be giving as the angels give.'* George MacDonald

❝ *'You give but little when you give of your possessions. It is when you give of yourself that you truly give.'* Khalil Gibran

Be generous and you will reap benefits in full, generous measure. This is a law of the universe, including love and life. It may not happen in the same way, or the way you immediately want, but when you give abundantly in terms of love and life and an inner glow of happiness – and in ways you may never see – you will generously, abundantly be blessed. Generosity is of the essence of a happy relationship and generosity goes round the world too. Just like a smile or kindness, it will light up your heart and even if not received generously by your partner in the moment, will nevertheless radiate out through your life and into theirs and others. It needs to be freely given. Thinking of what you'll receive back is kind of mean and so doesn't help. Just do it – be it – live it.

It starts with being thankful. Give thanks to the universe or your God for all your blessings and pretty soon you'll be thanking your partner for being there, for being their self, for being with you and loving you and doing things for you. And you'll be giving thanks, too, that you are generous and enjoy being there for them, for your love, for your impulse to do things for them, and spend time with them and generally live and love with them.

When we're mean, we feel horrible and it taints our view of everything. Mean-spirited, we wither. Thankful and generous, you thrive, expand, develop. Above all you love. For generosity is all about love – loving yourself first of all; that's important for if you don't love yourself how are you to love others? And about loving life, the people in your life and especially your partner and the wonder of it all.

Generosity is big-hearted – it lifts you up and opens your hearts. It's capacious too – your capacity for giving grows and grows. As ever, it's a matter of practise. When you remember to make it your practice, your relationship will respond in the loveliest of ways as you enjoy, together, a generous life of fun and love and action and friendship and peace.

BE GENEROUS IN YOUR THANKS

Generosity is linked to a thankful attitude. Feeling munificent you can live and love abundantly.

Start each day with thanks. When you wake up instead of feeling grouchy and wishing you could go back to sleep, or full of dread for the day ahead, switch off those feelings and list some of your blessings. Little things, big things – whatever comes to mind, and including your partner and all the love in your life as well as between the two of you. In your mind say a willing, joyous thank you. Sounds difficult? Just try it – as you start to think of the many things you have to be thankful for, your mood will start to lighten. It's a genuinely feel-good practice and it triggers a positive attitude for the whole day, including towards your partner. You two people fell in love, got together and have stayed together. Even in difficult times, your love is there – you wouldn't be bothering to read this if not. Be glad. Give thanks. Generously.

And see over the next few days as you make this your practice the positive effect this has on your interaction in all kinds of subtle and obvious ways.

BE GENEROUS IN YOUR ACTIONS

You know how good it is when you meet a 'Yes Person'? Someone who's willing to give suggestions a positive consideration; someone who will say 'Yes I can help' whenever possible; someone who makes time for you? It's just the same for you and your partner; it makes life sweeter, easier and generally encourages you to love each other all the more. So just for today try it out. Instead of digging your heels in as a matter of routine, opt out of that routine and try saying 'Yes, can do', or at least 'Yes, that's a good idea, I'll think about it'. If you're prone to being reluctant to make love much of the time, next time they're up for it and you're not, instead think to yourself 'Hey – I know I'll enjoy it once we get going, and what's half an hour out of my life?' and take your partner by the hand and lead them into the bedroom. And any positive impulse you have to do something nice for them – those random acts of kindness again – go ahead, say yes to it. At the end of the day enjoy looking back and realizing how much more pleasantly it's run and how good you feel because of your generosity in saying 'Yes'. Suggest they try it too. Have fun with it (remember of course it doesn't mean you have to say 'Yes' to everything!) and see how it lights and spices you both up.

BE GENEROUS WITH YOUR SELF

Willingly give your partner your time, your affection, your inner self.

Money and things are easy to give when we have them. The thought is nice, of course, but what I ask you to give is the most valuable gift of all – be generous with your self. Make time to be with your partner, to give up a little of the independence you've struggled to achieve, to give your affection and be generous too in intimacy – emotional and physical. It can be a lot easier to be detached – it takes generosity to connect as it takes a part of you. So try stretching your boundaries and being loving in a very 'you' way – your time, your personality, all freely given as an expression of your love. And be generous in receiving your partner's love and attention. Don't brush each other off, always saying 'I'm too busy' or 'I want to work', or whatever excuses you use to fail to engage with each other. Meet each other halfway and hug – emotionally and physically. Now and then – certainly often – give of yourselves.

Putting it all together

Love and attention, generously given, are like nectar for happiness – nutritious, energy giving, delicious – a truly feelgood elixir of life. It can seem a hard idea to give of your self when your life is already full to bursting – but the magic of it is that in giving as though you have abundant resources of time and love to give your partner, you will have. Often of course it's about quality, not quantity, and about being there for each other in the moment, full on and vibrant in your love and responsiveness and in your commitment and support. Be munificent with them at least for some time every day – and many days much more often.

It feels so much better for yourself as well as your partner. When we are mean with our time, love, attention and thoughtfulness it always turns the meanness back on our own self. When we're mean we feel mean and it's a miserable, miserly feeling. Be generous, on the other hand, and you'll feel warm and kind and bountiful. And who better to give of yourself generously than to the partner you love? Open yourself up to them and generously, lovingly, unsparingly value each other and your relationship. Happiness is an active thing – it needs your mutual input and your recognition. It needs the two of you connecting, generously – and when you do, it will flow in generous measure in all kinds of ways.

15 Keep attraction vibrant

> ❝ 'Few people dare now to say that two beings have fallen in love because they have looked at each other. Yet it is in this way that love begins, and in this way only.' Victor Hugo

> ❝ 'No matter what a woman looks like, if she's confident, she's sexy.' Paris Hilton

> ❝ 'Zest is the secret of all beauty. There is no beauty that is attractive without zest.' Christian Dior

> ❝ 'A pleasant voice, which has to include clear enunciation, is not only attractive to those who hear it... its appeal is permanent.' Loretta Young

> ❝ 'Taking care of your appearance and staying interested in each other's lives and thoughts is a compliment that keeps the spark sparkling.' Rosie Hallett

It's easy to grow complacent about attraction. In the beginning you fancy each other like mad. Each of you thinks the other's the most gorgeous person – to them – on the planet. You like each other's looks, smell, personality, voice, touch, sense of humour and – well, just about everything turns you on. This wild, passionate phase plateaus out in time – but the attraction is still strong. You like being up close, looking into each other's eyes, being around each other generally, and there are still moments, many, when that pull, that intense attraction strengthens and carries you both up and away. This is actually as lovely a phase as the earlier one. You're relaxed together, confident and comfortable.

And this can last a lifetime. It simply – like just about everything else good in life – needs some attention from you both and some tender loving care. All the Secrets help keep you and the love you share vibrant and strong – they are all about thinking of each other and so is attraction. It's about consideration for the other person. You're all the time noticing each other – how you are, how you look, how you're connecting – or not. Awareness of this keeps us on our toes – just as we were when we first met.

So now, as then, be keen and glad to make a good impression. Letting things slide signals waning interest not just in oneself but in your partner. Self-interest and respect and interest in them is vital. It signals continuing love, as does paying attention to your looks – your skin, your clothes, the way you hold yourself. Taking care of your health is important too – a Secret in itself (Secret 50). Respect and consideration are the opposite of neglect and they both nurture and enrich the way you feel about yourselves and each other.

They say familiarity breeds contempt but I don't think that's true. Familiarity holds hands with intimacy and the two together are one of the loveliest things about a good relationship. Just make sure it doesn't morph into disrespect and neglect of how you're coming across and how they're feeling about you. Be as good as you can be in looks and vibrancy and the mystery of attraction will keep the magic of your attraction sparkling all your life together.

TAKE CARE OF THE PHYSICAL ELEMENTS OF ATTRACTION

It sounds so obvious yet you only have to look around at others to see how easy it is to let ourselves go. So keep yourself together. It's a compliment to your partner, showing you want to be attractive to them.

It isn't just about clothes, but yes, they are important. Your clothes are an expression of you, your personality, your essence. Even if you're on a budget, keep dressing well. Should you dress to please your partner? There are so many discussions about this. I think it's up to you. A good compromise if you like to choose your own style, but they like certain other clothes is to have a few things they like that you do too. They'll be pleased when you wear them — a compliment that will attract them and their compliments. Keep looking good in each other's eyes — a simple Secret but powerful in continuing attraction.

Take care of your body too. Again — this is about self-value and confidence which, like a well-cared-for physique, is compelling. A well-cared-for soul and mind are also intrinsically attractive. Personal laziness is all about neglect — of oneself, our partner, relationship and life. Taking care of yourself feels good.

BE SENSITIVE TO YOUR MUTUAL PHYSICAL ATTRACTION

In the worst scenario — the one with the less-often sexual need — either one has sex even when they don't feel like it to avoid displeasing their partner, or shows clearly they're not up for it, or makes an excuse. This leads to frustration and feelings of rejection or pressure. There is another way that happily bridges the difference. It's to understand each other's right to feel as they do and be as they are and agree to meet somewhere in the middle. Pressure to have sex simply turns you away even more, physically and emotionally. Considerate acceptance with no sulking or further asking whatsoever makes both feel more loving towards each other and, very often, encourages desire another time.

A plan helps too. Prescribed love-making may seem like a contradiction in terms, but it's surprisingly sexy to care for and encourage your mutual attraction. For instance your agreement might be to make love once at the weekend and once during the week at a roughly agreed time. You agree to put your all into it at these times and the reward for both is truly satisfying sex that's well worth compromising for. Sensitivity and quality win hands-down over insistence and quantity. It's also a good idea to have a signal for 'yes I'd love to — let's!' and if one doesn't respond with the same signal, you implicitly agree not to, no questions asked. Again, it takes the pressure off and frees you for genuine desire another time.

STAY INTERESTING TO EACH OTHER

Keep vibrant in your own mind and actions and be interested in your partner's. A big part of attraction is to the mind. You could have a drop-dead gorgeous man or woman in front of you, wanting you, but if you weren't interested in them as a person you probably wouldn't be interested in them sexually for long, if at all. Sexual attraction is mostly in the mind – it starts with a thought in your mind and continues with a certain fascination with your partner's mind. Keep this wonderful rapport flourishing by keeping yourselves interesting and, importantly, consciously maintaining your interest in each other. Confidence is a very fanciable trait, and so is positivity – a vibrant upbeat attitude to life is magnetically appealing too. All these are Secrets of happiness in their own right and, activated by love, they come together in a special alchemy in sexual desire. Mix the magic and enjoy.

Putting it all together

Desire is a complex mix of physical and mental attraction. It's a given when you fall in love and, with a little ongoing input from both of you, can always be as the years go by. Take care of it by taking care of yourselves and your sexual and sensual interaction. Look after your looks – your bodies, your faces, your health. Of course we change as we mature, but we can always treasure our skin, our muscle tone, our hair to the best of our ability. Our minds can actually keep improving throughout our lives – the key is to make sure we keep our brains active and live interesting lives too. One of the keys to the Secret of attraction is to maintain a keen interest in each other's mind and to keep appreciating each other's body too. It stokes love, keeping it vibrant and visceral.

It's so important to stay attractive to each other. When you are you'll actively want to spend time together, you'll enjoy looking at each other, talking and generally enjoying life together. Stay attractive and you take care of the chemistry between you in so many ways. Not least, knowing you're attractive to each other is a pleasure in itself. Being attractive to your partner and being attracted by them – this is all part of happiness together.

Zest in life and the love you share and in your magnetism for each other is charismatically attractive. Love each other and live it!

16) Embrace intimacy

'Enlightenment is the key to everything, and it is the key to intimacy, because it is the goal of true authenticity.'
Marianne Williamson

'To want both intimacy and independence... is a difficult line to walk, yet both needs are important to a marriage.'
Hedy Lamarr

'Among men, sex sometimes results in intimacy; among women, intimacy sometimes results in sex.' Barbara Cartland

'There's nothing more intimate in life than simply being understood. And understanding someone else.' Brad Meltzer

'The opposite of loneliness is not togetherness, it's intimacy.'
Richard Bach

Intimacy is about knowing each other and in that knowing coming close. It can, particularly if we don't know ourselves well, be difficult to let go of our sense of self-consciousness and protectiveness. We can wrap a fear of intimacy around us and use it as a shield. But only in letting such defences down can you truly get to know your partner, and they you, in the deepest, most enriching depth and breadth possible. And when you do that you give love a chance to grow and thrive exponentially.

Intimacy can come into our emotional, physical and sexual contact, weaving its magic in and between all three. It's not the same as familiarity – for one thing it never breeds contempt! It is an always respectful knowledge of your own truth and a willingness to share it, and a willingness, too, to learn about your partner – their being, their fears and braveness, their ideas, their intelligence, their frailty. It's a love of their beauty too, body and soul – and their potential for more. Allowing and enjoying intimacy is also a way of honouring each other the best way two people can, bringing your minds, bodies and emotions into this loveliest of equations.

Intimacy develops through communication and understanding. It can seem to deepen swiftly in quantum leaps and bounds, and it can come in the subtlest of small steps, accumulating over the years in the richest seam of loving imaginable. It is in itself a thing of beauty, a treasure of and around your relationship that no one can take from you. It feels good and it's wholesome, never sullied, nor cheaply or carelessly summoned. It comes of love and a wanting and willingness to let that love expand and deepen and flourish inwardly and outwardly.

Intimacy is a magical part of a relationship and intrinsic to lasting happiness between you.

So let go of any fears and inhibitions that prevent you from sharing your self-knowledge of each other and your individual quest for it, and say yes to closeness of the kind that draws you together in love, warmth and understanding.

DECIDE TO ALLOW AND ENABLE MORE INTIMACY WITH YOUR PARTNER

To encourage intimacy it helps to think of the benefits it will give you both: a special kind of rapport that deepens the feeling of being a team; a sense of being lovingly connected, mind, body and soul; far fewer disputes and the ability to manage without lasting rancour any that do arise. Think, too, of the deeper knowledge it will give you of yourselves as well as each other. Above all, imagine the wonderful feeling of letting go of inhibition and sharing intimacy – when you do this you are halfway there already. It starts with a decision. Decide to bring it about!

Just making the decision to allow and enjoy intimacy between you goes a long way to shaking off any inhibitions about doing so. Think to yourself, if any still hold you back: 'Intimacy isn't just a good idea between two people who love each other, it's a great one.' You are two people who love each other. Dismantle the barriers between you. Look at each other with love and draw close emotionally.

FORGIVE ANY GRIEVANCES

It's far easier to enjoy intimacy if you let go of grievances. It's saying – in your minds or, if you like, aloud: 'Let's forgive ourselves and each other for any wrongs we've done and hurts we've given. Really forgive, right now.' And actually, consciously, do just that. Feel all the hurt, guilt and blame you've ever felt dropping away from you. As I write, I have a sensation of stretching my neck and spine and feeling the freedom forgiveness gives. (More on this in Secret 25.) Appreciate how good it is to be free of all that negativity. Imagine that you can now give each other love – deep, wonderful love – unreservedly. Just do it. And now – and every day – express this love in gestures. Smile with your mind and eyes as well as your mouth, hug mindfully with love, be thoughtful in all kinds of ways for each other's home comforts. Give of yourselves and appreciate each other's gift to you.

LET YOURSELVES ENJOY BEING TACTILE

Touch is a wonderful part of intimacy and this powerful exercise will free you of any resistance you might have to sharing touch:

Stand facing each other and look into each other's eyes. Hold your gaze for several seconds – maybe a whole minute. Let any embarrassment come and go; you may grimace or laugh (that's fine), but keep your eye contact constant. Then take turns to touch each other's face. Gently feel the skin, shape and features. You perhaps won't have done this since you were first in love. Feel the sense of wonder you did then that you are with this amazing person, loving them, appreciating their beauty and belovedness.

Now hug each other and hold the hug for a few seconds – or as long as you like – longer than you would normally hug each other. Feel, again, the wonder of being close like this with the person you love.

Encourage yourselves to enjoy physical closeness often, mindfully, appreciatively and always feeling the wonder of it. Love the way their touch feels and the way it feels to touch them. Love the scent of them too. Enjoy it all. Don't assume it will lead to sexual or sensual intimacy (see Secret 7). Enjoy it in its own right. Tactile intimacy with the partner you love is one of life's most amazing gifts.

Putting it all together

Togetherness is good but intimacy is in another realm of closeness. When you open your truth to each other – letting each other in on your inner knowledge of your being, your soul, your feelings – you open yourselves to the deepest understanding, bringing with it a sublime feeling of closeness and a love that is like nothing else. It starts and continues with ongoing forgiveness. Of course feelings of hurt, whether caused by your partner or by previous partners or others, can always spontaneously recur – but so can the process of forgiving. Keeping a forgiving mindset enables you to enter willingly into intimacy. When you have held back from getting too close, that first step can seem huge – but with self-understanding and a wish to make and enjoy the very best and deepest of connections with each other, it's doable.

Today, we are so used to being independent and guarding our autonomy fiercely that it can seem very strange to let others into our innermost space. It helps to remember that intimacy doesn't mean letting go of your independence, far from it, in fact, because in intimacy you will understand each other better and want to protect each other's right to be individual. But once you make the decision to let go of inhibitions and go for it, and then reach out to each other to grow closer emotionally and physically, it's like a benediction. It just feels very good. Supremely good. Be close – and enjoy.

17 Respect each other

> **''** 'Everyone should be respected as an individual, but no one idolized.' Albert Einstein

> **''** 'One of the most sincere forms of respect is actually listening to what another has to say.' Bryant H. McGill

> **''** 'The bond that links your true family is not one of blood, but of respect and joy in each other's life.' Richard Bach

> **''** 'Respect is one of the greatest expressions of love.' Miguel Ángel Ruiz

> **''** 'To be sensual, I think, is to respect and rejoice in the force of life, of life itself, and to be present in all that one does, from the effort of loving to the making of bread.' James A. Baldwin

The word respect has different meanings, but in the context of a happy relationship, it's respect in the sense of appreciating and valuing each other and your own selves, so you have both a healthy self-respect and mutual respect.

This translates in many kinds of behaviour. It's about being polite to each other, considerate for each other's feelings, sometimes being willing to defer to the other's opinion or decision, sometimes agreeing to take the lead. It's about balance and give and take, but always being thoughtful of the other's wellbeing as you pay kind, sensitive attention to each other.

As so often in the Secrets, mutual respect is something that's natural in the earliest stage of a relationship. Then, both of you are eager to impress with your courteous thoughtfulness. You're wary of upsetting your partner. You want to come across as well behaved, good mannered and keenly attentive. You take great care, in other words, of each other's feelings.

Do this all through your relationship, in every aspect, and most of the other Secrets will fall naturally and easily into place. They are conjoined and symbiotic in the best of ways.

The greatest enemy of respect is overfamiliarity. As we saw in the last Secret (Secret 16), familiarity is not the same as intimacy. The former can easily lapse over into disrespect and even boredom and/or antipathy, while intimacy nurtures love, mutual thoughtfulness and an ongoing interest in and attraction to each other.

It's very easy to be seduced by what starts as a lovely feeling as you grow familiar with each other's personality, only to become complacent about looking out for each other's dignity and self-esteem. But it's never too late to remember how important it is to be watchful for disrespect. It can slide into your relationship in different ways, and we'll look next at strategies to guard against this and transform it back to mutual regard and carefulness of each other.

Think love and it's a great catalyst. The minute love comes to the forefront of your mind, it's obvious that being considerate to your partner is the right thing and that it feels so much better, for you both, than the opposite.

LOOK AFTER YOUR OWN AND EACH OTHER'S SELF-RESPECT

When your self-esteem is high, it automatically attracts the same attitude from others. So be careful not to get into the habit of being self-deprecating or allowing your partner to put you down. Both often come veiled as humorous but like other kinds of negative humour – for instance sarcasm – all it does is encourage disrespect and even dislike. People, your partner included, are likely to take you at your own valuation, and the more your partner puts you down, even if they call it 'teasing', the more you are likely to believe them and think you're pretty useless. Encourage each other to believe in yourselves and you'll encourage each other to be and do the best you can.

Don't shout at each other, even during a dispute. You wouldn't shout at a friend or colleague, so why your partner? Talk, discuss and, for sure, stand up for yourself, but always, always, always with mutual respect.

BE ACTIVE IN RESPECTING EACH OTHER

Disrespect is born of laziness so beware neglecting each other, being offhand or failing to listen and instead put some energy into being actively caring. Show you think well of your partner by doing things for them thoughtfully and in your general attitude to them. Encourage them to have high self-esteem and they will think well of you and their respect for you will thrive too. Just as disrespect often comes from neglect and thoughtlessness, so respect comes from an attitude of consideration.

It's necessary, in just the same way, to deliberately decide to show respect for each other on a constant and ongoing basis as otherwise, however indeliberately, your relationship could unwittingly slide into one of mutual disrespect. When a couple has ceased to be respectful and considerate of each other's feelings and wellbeing, they can soon come to despise and even scorn each other. A little thought and care, shown in everyday behaviour and attitude between you, is all it takes to keep a high regard for each other flourishing.

TALK EACH OTHER UP

In company on your own or as a couple only speak well of your partner. Carping about them is uncomfortable for others, even if they find such gossip titillating, and encourages a disrespectful attitude in you and them. I know it can be tempting to discuss your partner's faults and foibles with friends and even colleagues, but it can upset the balance of your respective relationships and negative griping and criticism is depressing, so inevitably dents relationship happiness. If you really need to talk to someone, seek out a counsellor or wise person who doesn't know you or your partner personally and so can be objective. When socializing, the old adage, 'if you can't say something nice about someone, don't say anything at all' is never truer than when referring to your partner.

Putting it all together

We see disrespect in relationships in TV dramas, on news clips, among people we know. It sets a really bad example and can be infectious – it's easy to find yourself copying negative behaviour as though it's the norm. It isn't; it's insidiously depressing and can wreck a relationship.

If you were lucky, you grew up with parents who not only loved each other, but who behaved lovingly towards each other. If not, imagine for a moment how good it would have been (or be if they're still together) if they weren't mean to and about each other. It feels so fantastic for kids if their parents behave with respect and it's a great and very comfortable and inspiring example for everyone. Now visualize being in a supermarket next to a couple you don't know. Imagine first that they are shouting or grumbling at each other. You feel they despise and dislike each other, don't you, and you pick up on how bad that makes them both feel? Now visualize the opposite. The couple speak warmly, kindly and courteously. You immediately feel the love that shines between them. It makes you feel good and you know without doubt how happy they are.

Remember this if ever you are tempted to be horrid or snide to your partner and choose instead to be warmly well-mannered and courteous. Remind them to be respectful to and about you, too. Think love and, like the positive couple in the supermarket, behave as though you love each other. Ask for their respect, and give them yours. And feel the happiness that flows. It's easy to do – but it feels like pure magic.

18 Share enjoyment of food

‘One cannot think well, love well, sleep well, if one has not dined well.’ Virginia Woolf

‘After a good dinner one can forgive anybody, even one's own relations.’ Oscar Wilde

‘Cooking for someone, sharing and enjoying the meal, draws you close and fills you both with happiness as well as the food.’ Rosie Hallett

‘Eating together is all about love.’ Joan Rench

‘A smiling face is half the meal.’ Proverb

The pleasures of eating together draw you together. The Secret of the happiness it brings isn't what you eat – it's your mutual enthusiasm. Loving your food, feeling appreciative of it, being glad to be together enjoying it – all this is seductive, luring you both in the nicest of ways to appreciating each other's company. One of the first signs of interest when you've just met is an invitation to a meal. In sharing one of the simplest yet greatest pleasures of life, we relax, exchange ideas, explore how much we like each other. There's the opportunity for lots of eye contact too as you talk. Mmm – enjoying food together is like a magnet – if attraction is present, it will intensify it. It can also be seductive in the sexual sense. Eating with great relish is a sign of a passionate nature, and sharing sensations of lovely tastes and delighting in the pleasure of eating is very sexy.

Then there's the compliment you give each other when you organize yourselves and take the time to eat together. It shows you value the chance and space not just to share the enjoyment of a meal but to chat about the day you've had and to catch up on home and family matters.

If you treat shared meals as an oasis of relaxation, pleasure, connection and wellbeing, it's a haven of respite in the day.

There are other gifts, too. You can take pleasure in all aspects of preparing and cooking a meal you'll share. If you think of your partner when you're shopping for a meal you'll share together, it adds another dimension to what otherwise might be a mundane experience. Eating together, at every stage, is an expression of love and a chance to show your appreciation of each other.

Food shared is more than fuel for the body – it's nourishment for your souls and your relationship. It continues your romance – just as when you first dined together, it draws you close and lets your attraction sing.

All in all, it scores very highly in your mutual happiness together.

APPRECIATE EVERY STAGE OF A MEAL TOGETHER

Appreciation begins with planning the meal and choosing ingredients and recipes you both like or would like to try. As you go round the supermarket, think of what your partner and you will enjoy and imagine the tastes and pleasure. Prepare the food with love – give thanks for it, aware of how lucky we are to have enough food and so much choice and high quality.

Preparing food in many cultures is a kind of spiritual and even sacred ritual and we, too, can let the ritual give us a warm feeling of love and abundance. Remember that you don't necessarily need elaborate or highly spiced dishes. The more you salt and spice, the less responsive your palate will become. Often, the simplest of food, if of high quality (like good but simple lovemaking), is the most delicious and rewarding, and if you pay attention to the subtlety of the taste you'll begin to reset your palates for this appreciation. Share in your pleasure at every stage – enthusiasm makes you both feel happy. Set the table with care too – knowing it's ready and looks nice is inviting and relaxing and the fact you've taken the trouble is a compliment to you both. I find it hugely helpful to clear up and wash up as I cook – that way there's no build-up of pots and pans to tackle afterwards.

GUARD MEALTIMES AS A SPECIAL OASIS OF TOGETHERNESS

Make every meal you share an oasis of love. Meals are a chance to relax and enjoy each other's company and share your pleasure in the food too. Value it to the full as an important opportunity to catch up with each other's day, thoughts and ideas. Listen as well as talk. Agree not to discuss finances or any stressful issues at the table, ever. Eating needs to be stress free – digestion isn't helped by too much adrenaline! It's good, too, to know that this is a stress-free zone – it's a time of healing as well as nourishment and something you can always look forward to and enjoy.

Remember to eat slowly – this is so important to enjoyment (as well as digestion!). If one of you bolts your food, it's as though you want the shared meal to be over as quickly as possible. Put your cutlery down between each mouthful, chew well and appreciatively and let the meal stretch out. It's a key part of the day, and your relationship. Fill it with shared enjoyment, mutual regard and love and it will give you an abundance of dividends in couple happiness.

ENJOY YOUR FOOD

People often moan about what a bother the preparation of meals are. But that's just an attitude of mind, so make them a pleasure instead. Sharing, as ever, is important though. Different people like different things and you will need to work out as a couple the balance of domestic tasks, including meal preparation, that's right for you. You may share it all, or perhaps one of you would rather not be involved in the preparation while you like it, in which case they can input into the domestic responsibilities in other ways, like DIY or paying for help. Any domestic work should be willingly done with as much enjoyment as possible, so it's essential that it's fair to both of you. It goes without saying but do remember, both of you, not to spoil your appetite before a meal. If you're eating together in the evening, for instance, give afternoon or early snacks a miss. That way you can enjoy the food you share to the full.

Putting it all together

Love and food share a lot in common and are very good shared, too. They thrive with willingness, eagerness, appreciation and proactive enjoyment. All of these attitudes start with a thought, and you can choose to be positive or negative. When you positively want to love your partner you're halfway there – you'll think of all the lovely things about them and in behaving lovingly they'll most likely be loving back and there you are – happiness on a plate. Same with food – emotionally as well as literally. If you both decide to savour every mouthful, take your time and enjoy every minute of this special time together and the opportunity to talk, you will. Like love, appreciative eating feels wonderful. Both are good for your health – mind, body and spirit. Together they enhance each other. So just as you made eating together part of the romance of falling in love, make it part of the romance, now, of choosing to stay together as a couple through the years. Let mealtimes keep you close – using the opportunity to connect and communicate in shared pleasure to stay in touch, up to date in knowing each other. Use it to pay attention to each other and to appreciate what gorgeous, sensual and passionate people you both are. Make the space, every day if possible and at least several times a week, to take the time and savour the food you enjoy together – and the love.

19 Accept and tolerate

CC *'As I've gotten older, I've had more of a tendency to look for people who live by kindness, tolerance, compassion, a gentler way of looking at things.'* Martin Scorsese

CC *'When travelling with someone, take large doses of patience and tolerance with your morning coffee.'* Helen Hayes

CC *'It is tolerance that is the source of peace, and intolerance that is the source of disorder and squabbling.'* Pierre Bayle

CC *'Compassion and tolerance are not a sign of weakness, but a sign of strength.'* Dalai Lama

CC *'I don't think it's good to try and change anyone. The trick and the mystery – of relationships and life in general – is to learn to live with the bits you don't like.'* Helen Mirren

The Secret of tolerance in a relationship is about respecting each other's right to differ in opinions, feelings and ways of doing things. It absolutely doesn't mean tolerating bad or abusive behaviour in a relationship.

You and your partner each emerged from your respective upbringing with a set of notions and habits that can feel pretty much set in stone. It can cause puzzlement, confusion and probably many a frustration too. The key to solving problems of differing opinions, feelings and behaviour is to remember it's down to your upbringing. Instantly, you're set to be more tolerant and instantly you'll feel less bothered by the difference and far more accepting.

Tolerance is no sign of weakness – it shows individuality and character strength because it requires you to think independently. It's one of the most vital secrets of a happy relationship because without it you'd forever be clashing and trying to change each other. With it, you'll get along, not always agreeing but accepting that you have some different ways and that this is totally natural and not a bad thing.

Think about the opposite: if your partner opted, or felt forced, to do everything you do the way you do it, wouldn't you end up pitying or despising them and getting rather bored? And if you melded yourself totally into their ways, wouldn't you feel spineless and uninteresting, and somewhere deep down resent that they weren't interested in the real you? Isn't it much more interesting that you each retain your individuality? It's all a fine balance. In Secret 39 we look at the magic of compromise and in Secret 46 the fun of developing shared interests. All are different takes but work well alongside each other in a spirit of give and take.

Tolerance and acceptance give a relationship flow, helping you skate smoothly together through life in a way that works very well and feels wonderful. Even when you don't and perhaps will never agree on a particular issue, together they ditch frustration in one fell swoop and give you peace and concord.

ACCEPT YOU'RE DIFFERENT AND FIND A COMMON LANGUAGE

It really does feel sometimes as though men and women are from different planets. Again, just remembering that there actually is a genetic difference in our brains enables you to smile tolerantly and say 'Ah, bless them – they're just different!' Then, instead of grouchily accusing them of 'You just don't get it!' or 'Why can't you understand how I feel!' you'll accept that they don't and can't, at least in the way you've been stating your case. Now tell them how you feel in a way they can understand, or at least accept. To help, speak gently, if possible with a sense of humour, and explain your feelings without blaming or shaming them. It's well-known advice that rather than accusingly saying 'You make me feel xxx', which would put them on the defensive, it's far better and un-inflammatory to say 'When you do so and so, I feel xxx'. They can then reflect on this cause and effect and tolerance and acceptance should follow, even if understanding doesn't.

DEAL EFFECTIVELY WITH ANNOYING PERSONAL HABITS

Personal habits are one of the biggest causes of annoyance and potential dislike between partners and even those traits that first endeared you may wear thin as time goes by. Remembering it didn't niggle then is a good way to renew that tolerance. Another is to shrug your shoulders and let the irritation drop off you. Is it really, when the chips are down, that important? If not, accept they'll probably always do it and reckon that you may as well not get indignant about it. If it's something that would revolt anyone, then tell them clearly, as sensitively as possible. Often we're unaware of habits altogether, or that one of them is repellent to other people. We may not much like being told, but as long as the telling is straightforward and not unkind, we soon see it's something that needs our attention and willpower to stop. But provided your individual habits aren't socially unacceptable, tolerance and acceptance will allow you to dismiss any irritation about each other's and pretty soon you won't even notice them. We all have a few warts – love doesn't fret about them.

AVOID THE TEMPTATION TO TRY TO CHANGE EACH OTHER

How prone we are to trying to change our partners! But the personality you each have is your individual blueprint, the one you fell in love with when first together. So why try to change them? Think about this next time you're tempted to. Would you really want them to morph into someone they're not? Be glad for their authenticity and encourage them to be the best person they can, just as you want them to love you the way you are and encourage you to shine too. (See Secrets 26 and 37 for more on this.)

Taking an interest in the psychology behind your initial attraction can be interesting and therapeutic in renewed acceptance. Generally, we choose potential partners because they're similar to us – in looks, background and personality. Remember how comfortable and good this felt. But if the slightest bit bored, liven up your relationship occasionally – do something different and excite yourselves and each other! But it's also possible to be attracted because you're very different – opposites even. The magnetism is still there – feel it, appreciate it and let it energize your love while enjoying bridging the gap – the coming together accentuated and as wondrous as when you first fell in love.

Putting it all together

Kindness and compassion make a relationship great – and tolerance is a big part of this. Manipulation, on the other hand, is destined to be frustrating and unsettling for both of you. If your partner has developed an anti-social or obsessive habit then help them see this and control or drop it. Otherwise, remember that you loved them initially, warts and all, and they are still the same flawed, sometimes annoying but above all attractive-to-you person. Love always needs tending – we don't love unconditionally but it's unreasonable to keep adding conditions. When you settled down together you tacitly accepted each other's shortcomings. Remember that tolerance and acceptance are not signs of weakness and are never about accepting bad behaviour. They are about strength of character; on an ongoing basis we choose to love and this entails accepting the whole person and tolerating the flaws they, like you, like all of us, have. Anyone can be annoying. Anyone can choose not to be annoyed. A partnership is a love affair in the long term and acceptance and tolerance are the lubricants that keep love flowing easily – they are great blessings. They are your choice.

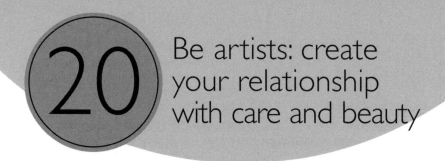

20 Be artists: create your relationship with care and beauty

'Relationship is an art.' Miguel Ángel Ruiz

'Life – and love – is a work in progress.' Shakti Gawain

'Most people forget that you have to create relationships. The allure of the first years settles down, and at that moment, you better start creating it; otherwise, you're going to lose out.'
John Travolta

'Like everything else in this world, a relationship is made of small building blocks and the couple puts them together in their own way to make the togetherness that's right for them.'
Rosie Hallett

'I think "making it up as you go along" is one of the greatest, and most important processes of any age. No great explorer set out with a detailed set of explorer guidelines. They adjusted and discovered.' Eric Reiss

Your relationship started with the two of you falling in love and realizing you wanted to be together. But you probably had precious little, if any, teaching or preparation for this life-changing agreement and way of living. Most of us imagine in those early days of love that it will always be spontaneous. But every relationship is an artwork and one that's always in progress, for it lives as long as you both live and stay together, and every day is new and different.

So every day you are creating how you live, the way you get on and the way you love each other. The things you do and say, the way you are together, your readiness to adapt to each other's phases and stages of life – all this forms a picture – an ever-changing painting of your love and togetherness.

Emotions vary hugely too – at various times you'll feel happy, sad, joyous, wretched, improving, failing, sailing, grounded. Things happen beyond our control, of course. Some things you can make happen but sometimes you might be stuck within certain circumstances. But you can always choose how you react because you can choose to react positively or negatively and so you to a large extent create your relationship, day by day, in your style.

So your relationship is in a sense a work of art of which you are the creators. Great art is a positive choice, proactive, hopeful, challenging and often thrilling, and when undertaken in an ongoing positive spirit, immensely satisfying. Your relationship, viewed positively and lovingly by you both is a work of art in its own right and part of the artwork of life too. It's made up of myriad gestures and actions – brushstrokes of togetherness, marks of love and beauty and, sometimes dark feelings but if you're caring of the whole picture, coming together into a relationship that's good, enjoyable and inspiring.

To a large extent we paint the life we want and you and your partner are the creators of your relationship – no one else, just the two of you. You can use all your knowledge, techniques and gut feeling. You can snatch inspiration from the air around you. You can enthuse and encourage each other. It is yours to make and yours to joy in.

TREAT YOUR RELATIONSHIP AS A LIVING, CHANGING THING

Remember that your interaction is always ever-changing as you and your partner react to each other and your individual and shared lives. You both have a huge influence on it so never feel stuck – together you can steer it the way that's right for you. Think how you would like your rapport to be and the kind of life you would like too. Imagine a day in the life of your relationship and jot down how it will progress from waking up together to going to sleep last thing. Now think of what you do like about your relationship and how you tend to spend a weekend day. If you realize the imaginary and real versions aren't too far apart give thanks – you're already doing a great job in creating the kind of relationship you both want. But if not, don't worry, because if it's what you both want you can together adapt your usual routine to give you something much closer to the picture you'd ideally like.

Talk about this with your partner. Get them to do the exercise too and then have fun comparing notes. If there's some common ground, use it as a great start to merging your ideal leisure time together. If not, see how you can give a lot, take a little, to adjust and come up with a pattern that much pleases you both. Your leisure time, your love, your togetherness are just ingredients in your life – the two of you can mix them up the way you want. Try to converge your ideal days!

THINK CREATIVELY HOW YOU CAN WEAVE YOUR LIVES TOGETHER

On working days in your busy life it's important to make a special art of prioritizing each other and weaving your relationship through the fabric of everyday life so it stays rich and vibrant – a hugely enjoyable amalgamation of your interests and activities. Talk it over with your partner so you both stay aware of the plethora of distractions and make a point of liaising with each other at least at key points of the day and thinking of each other often at other times. Book some time to spend together, too, just the two of you. Do you need to book it? Yes I think it's important if you have busy schedules, to actually schedule in some you time in your diaries. That way you'll rarely let a day go by without coming together as a couple and having a chance to truly appreciate each other, one to one. You are both individually and as a couple important. Use your sizeable talent and energy to make this happen as part of the integrity and beauty of the artwork of your life. Can a relationship be beautiful? Absolutely – a relationship is the work of art you make it. As in anything creative, it's up to you to make it something truly lovely to be in.

MAKE YOUR PHYSICAL CONNECTIONS WITH EACH OTHER ATTRACTIVE TOO

Your bodies and your sexuality are to a large extent of your own making. Hone and tone your fitness and look after yourselves – not just for your own self but for each other – it's a huge compliment to your partner to stay as attractive as when you first met. While most of us enjoy relaxing now and then by slopping around, make an effort most of the time you're together to be sensually pleasing. Just as your life is an artwork, so are you as a being and, again, you are the creator of your intrinsic and outward beauty.

Appreciate and practise the art of creating an ongoing sexual rapport too. We think it will last for ever but actually it takes two to nurture mutual attraction very actively and positively right through the years as a lively part of your love. Be sexual, feel sexual and appreciate each other's wonderful sexuality. It's a gift to give and receive actively and positively with love at its heart.

Putting it all together

Don't make the mistake of assuming that life and love are things that just happen to you. Mostly they are, in many richly diverse respects, of your making. You and your partner are the creators of your relationship and as every day unfolds so the way you are together is brought into being by the two of you. Realize the joy of this. You are equipped and empowered to get on well and to keep your love flowing and strong. You evidently take an interest in this and want it very much – that's why you're reading this. So I know you have it in you to be the ongoing creators of something very special – a relationship that is a wonderfully comfortable, sometimes exciting, always full-of-love partnership in the best of senses. Just as a beautiful painting is created by the artist with passion, love and positivity stroke by stroke, mark by mark, step by step, so you and your partner create your life together, day by day. Make it loving and beautiful, sensual and rewarding. Above all, enjoy!

(21) Persevere

> 'We must have perseverance and above all confidence in ourselves. We must believe that we are gifted for something and that this thing must be attained.' Marie Curie

> 'The art of love is largely the art of persistence.' Albert Ellis

> 'A little more persistence, a little more effort, and what seemed hopeless failure may turn to glorious success.' Elbert Hubbard

> 'Problems are not stop signs, they are guidelines.' Robert H. Schuller

> 'Most people never run far enough on their first wind to find out they've got a second.' William James

Persevere is from the Latin 'perseverare' meaning 'continue steadfastly, persist'.

Despite our hopes and vows in the beginning, relationships don't always work out. More than half of UK marriages end in divorce and far more living-together partnerships bite the dust. Many things can go wrong, and if a couple truly find they are not compatible in the long term, I see no 'failure' in splitting up – it can be the sensible, positive way forward for both partners. But far too many who are compatible, who do love each other and who do have the potential to be very, very happy together needlessly give up. All the Secrets help avoid this sadness and show the way to staying happily together. But one of the most essential secrets of staying together, happily, for almost every couple is perseverance.

Separation and divorce are such an easy option that at the first sign of discord, or the first intimation that love and attraction are no longer automatic, they present themselves as a distinct possibility. Please, if this happens to you, take a step firmly back from this brink. Refuse to give up easily. Remember the good you share and very proactively think of all the positives of staying together happily. For happiness between you is as much a chosen option as separation.

In spite of everything, see yourselves determinedly as being on course for a continuing happy relationship. With any troublesome issues between you, decide to look for and expect a good outcome. This opens up the long vista of happiness and enables you to look for the way through to the long-term goal of staying together, congruently and compatibly.

Sometimes you'll feel as though you're taking one step forward and two back, but more often you'll keep taking forward steps – step by positive step as you stay on course. This is the heart of perseverance. You look at severance – at conflict and separation – and decide to determinedly avoid it and continue with hope, love and steadfastness.

I can't fool you that staying together is easy. But I can tell you it needn't be hard work and with both your hearts and heads in it, it can be wonderfully fulfilling. Just as when you pledged your love you believed your relationship the best, so it can continue. See it so. Make it so.

HOLD OUT FOR YOUR SECOND WIND

If you're worried you're no longer automatically 'in love', recognize that it's not the end of your relationship but the moving from phase one, the honeymoon months or years, into the main period of togetherness. The deepening, growing and ever expanding of love morphs into a true team partnership that can endure for ever and has its own huge benefits.

It's largely about pacing yourselves. You jumped in initially with great joy and everything sped along – your togetherness, your emotions, the whole thing of forging a life together had its own momentum. Then it stutters, a little at first, but becoming noticeably slower and less smooth. This is when it helps to think of yourselves as runners. Suddenly you're aware of the energy you're using to keep things going between you, and you can fear running out of steam altogether. You won't. You keep going. You run through the strain and stress. You forge on. And suddenly you'll find it's easy again. Your relationship breathes, you come close, all is well. From then on you maintain pace often effortlessly, sometimes with thought and great care. All the Secrets help and the more you put into it the more your love will grow and develop. You can help it mature well at a pace that's right for the two of you. All is well.

APPRECIATE THE VALUE OF BEING STEADFAST

There is a satisfaction about being steadfast. If ever you're tempted to defect from your relationship, think of this lovely word and what it means. Loyalty and the resolve to be together, to keep loving and caring for each other, this has an intrinsically wholesome value. It feels good to be faithful to each other and to the principle of solidarity. You are united and that's your choice. No one is forcing you – every day it's your decision. So determine to feel a purpose to hang on in there. Search in your hearts for the love that will make it not just possible but actually pretty blissful, because it is a kind of bliss to be with someone you love. Don't forget this love or get side-tracked from it – keep it to the forefront of your minds. And enjoy being steadfast in your love – a good committed relationship is one of the true treasures of this life.

So resolve to be faithful to each other with your minds as well as your bodies. Remember that being united is your ongoing choice and it's also your choice to enjoy remaking it every day. By willingly and enthusiastically committing to standing by each other you enable yourselves to relish your togetherness. A good relationship is one of the true treasures of life but only the two of you can work the magic that makes it so. Part of the magic is perseverance.

BE LOYAL IN YOUR MUTUAL ATTRACTION AND DESIRE FOR EACH OTHER

You hear people say sadly of their erstwhile partner: 'I suddenly fell out of love and then I didn't fancy them any more.' Truth is, it doesn't happen suddenly. If attraction and desire for each other are to remain vibrant, you need to keep practising them. So feel your love passionately as well as steadfastly. That might mean, for example, summoning the energy to make love when you're tired, having sex when your partner suggests it even though you're reading, remembering that once you get going you'll have a great time. It's bemusing that we stop practising so many of the things we actually love doing. We might say: 'I haven't time to play tennis/the piano/go dancing/write poetry, etc…' but this is just an excuse for not bothering, not making time, not keeping our interest keen. Enthusiasm comes in the doing with most things and it's never truer than with lovemaking and sex. Keep putting them off and you'll steadily lose the inclination until 'suddenly' it's no longer there. If you still fancy each other, that's brilliant. Start practising again, a little more often than you'd otherwise choose. Up the ante – bring it back into focus as a joy of your life together. Fancying each other and having great sex is one of life's greatest joys. Enjoy it! If you've stopped altogether it'll take more effort to get back the mutual attraction but you can. Counselling could help – but again it is practice and perseverance that brings back the magic and keeps it glowing. So put your hearts and minds into it.

No excuses or procrastinating – just choose to enjoy it and do, fulfillingly and lovingly. Make love for love of your partner and for your own pleasure and for a special sort of shared happiness that's very, very good.

Putting it all together

Perseverance is a bit of an old-fashioned concept today, but it's the glue that's held many a couple together through ups and downs. So often, problems are transitory, however desperate they feel in the moment. Time is a wonderful healer and also helps get things in perspective. You look back and wonder why you were so despondent or upset by this and that, realizing that in the whole patchwork of your relationship it wasn't nearly as significant as you then thought. And of course if you keep going, you have the chance to sort out differences, find ways through snags and reach compromises or other agreements.

So whenever you feel your happiness threatened, don't contemplate severance but keep the thought of renewed contentment with each other and your life together clearly in mind and steer determinedly towards it. Stand firm – steadfast and refuse to be daunted. Love is far tougher than we usually give it credit for and it can withstand any amount of turbulence given your mutual resolve, liberal amounts of affection and, last but not least, a sense of humour to lighten things up.

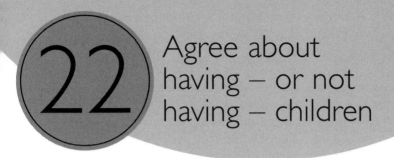

22 Agree about having – or not having – children

'It's important to remember that just because society pressures us to have children, we should listen to our instincts.' Michelle Rogerson

'As I grow older, I am more and more convinced that there are many roads to personal fulfilment – and that having children is not for everyone.' Garry Wilmore

'Having children is life-changing, to state the obvious. It's a gigantic shift in your life.' Thandie Newton

'Don't feel you have to or ought to have children. It's up to the two of you, no one else, and if you want your love to last you both need to feel the same way.' Joan Rench

'People often make the mistake of thinking having a baby will bring and hold them together but actually it can push you apart if one or both of you would rather not be a parent. You both need to have your hearts and heads in being parents – or not being parents – both can be good.' Anon

It's no Secret and I'll take it as a given that it's obviously great if you are in agreement when you decide to have or to not have a baby. This Secret of agreeing on parenthood is about the joy and comfort possible when you are parents and, whether or not by choice, when you don't have children.

For even when you are already in the situation, it's vital to accept your state of parenthood or non-parenthood and, together, put your all into enjoying this status quo. Mutual support is an ongoing thing that means the world when you're having regrets about having or not having kids – and most of us do have misgivings even when the initial decision was ours and we thought we'd always feel that way. I've talked to some parents who have admitted to me that they wish they hadn't had kids and some, too, who regret not having them, whether or not this was by choice. But the joyful thing is that the Secret of agreeing on parenting now, and as life goes by, can bring great happiness and one that not only brings you together over and over again, but does so right throughout your life. It's great for the children too.

What it means is that you face the situation and recognize how you feel about it and how your partner feels too. Then you can together decide to accept the way things are – being parents or not being parents – and instead of regrets, fill yourselves with positive thoughts and feelings about the situation. (For more on being parents, see the next Secret.) This way you don't waste any energy and time on wishing it were different or feeling frustrated or resentful that you are stuck as parents when you'd love to be free of the responsibility of kids, or stuck with being childless when you would have loved that responsibility. You look at the pros of your own situation and decide to maximize them and enjoy life to the hilt the way it is. As parents you unite to be the best parents you can and to enjoy it together. As non-parents you unite in loving the particular kind of freedom that being childless gives you. Instead of divisive negativity, positivity nurtures your love and gives you joy.

GRIEVE REGRETS ABOUT CHILDLESSNESS AND MOVE ON

If you regret not being parents, or not having another child, mourn the sadness of not having children or another one. Recognize it and feel it so that the grief is faced and lived. Having counselling can help a lot. But there comes a time to move on from regret, determinedly and courageously. Above all, refuse to feel bitter. Forgive the situation and what may seem like the unfairness of life and if your partner influenced you not to have kids, forgive them too. We can't always have what we want, but we can enjoy what we do have and it's much easier to feel the joy of life if we don't cloud ourselves with feelings of being hard done by. Sounds trite, but counting our blessings is a brilliant feel-good exercise. Then you can make the choice and keeping an ongoing commitment to love life as it is and each other as you did when you met and can continue to live and love together fulfillingly throughout the years.

IF YOU HAVE CHILDREN, FACE ANY REGRETS BUT ENJOY BEING PARENTS TOGETHER

Many parents occasionally envy the extra spending money and free time of those who don't and their freedom from the responsibility of being parents too. Be aware of any such feelings and don't feel guilty – they're very understandable however much parents adore their offspring. But deal with them firmly by immediately replacing them with the lovely things about having your children in your life. Let your love for them and the special kind of love you and your partner share as their parents suffuse you. It will if you just take a moment to let it. Put your all into being a great mum and dad and enjoy it with all your hearts. Remember that all parents have difficult times but they come and go and the joy surpasses all worries and sorrows.

ENJOY THE MANY BLESSINGS OF LIFE WHETHER OR NOT YOU ARE PARENTS

Today will pass and so will the years, all too quickly. Enjoy the present, fully aware how transitory it is and determine to enjoy the pluses, whatever your situation and appreciate and give thanks for all your good fortune. Whether or not you are parents, let your partner know that they are very, very important to you and you love them beyond words. If you have kids, enjoy the feeling of being a team in your parenting. Love the whole family feeling too and share the happiness it gives you both with each other. Show your partner your love in any of the countless ways you can and encourage them to show theirs by appreciating them and any gestures of love they make to you. Instead of regretting all that you don't have, be thankful for your many blessings.

Putting it all together

It's useless to waste the possibility of happiness on frustration or sadness about your parental state. Whether you are parents or non-parents there are pros and cons. Choose to see the pluses clearly and focus on them with all your positivity. This way you strengthen and nurture your relationship instead of sabotaging it with regrets and your love can continue to thrive. Enjoy it and enjoy each other. Remember that most people consider having a partner as one of life's greatest blessings. All couples start out loving each other and being aware of their good fortune in finding and falling for each other. The good fortune of you and your partner is still there – it's up to the two of you to appreciate it and look after it by being thankful and cherishing each other and your rapport. Children can strengthen your love and relationship – again it is your choice to make each other and the bond between you and the children your greatest priority and enjoy it. Not having children can also strengthen the bond between you just as much in its own way, creating a one-to-one togetherness that's very special.

Either way, the Secret is to dismiss regrets if and when they come to mind and choose to see – seeking them out if necessary – the good things about your relationship and also its additional potential. It is wonderful being parents – so many joys, so much love. Life is also great without children. It's up to you to recognize your good fortune and realize it by translating it into happiness. Let the love flow between you and your partner. Children or no children, it will shine!

23 Find solidarity as parents

66 'For important issues — before they take a stand with their child — parents should consult with each other. But for many day-to-day decisions, that is not workable. Each parent has a right to make on-the-fly decisions that they know will be backed.' Anthony E. Wolf

66 'If at all possible it's best to speak with one voice, otherwise it's confusing for the child and it could come between the two of you. Acting as equal partners, the spouses are sending a powerful message to the children which will help them to form equal partnerships themselves when they grow up.' Robin Skynner

66 'I think people have to really take a look at themselves and step back and say, "Our children are very important to us, so we need to come together on this." It's very important to come up with a cohesive plan to which you both adhere — or your child is liable to fall through the cracks of your lack of agreement.' James Lehman

66 'Present a united front with your children. If you feel that your spouse is disciplining (or failing to discipline) appropriately, do not take this up with the children. Take it up with your spouse afterwards, when the children are out of earshot. It is so important for kids to see their parents in agreement with one another, so that they know they cannot play you both against each other.' Sheila Wray Gregoire

'Hold regular catch-ups about the children so you can discuss approaches and ideas for dealing with problems. Focus on sharing the good things about parenting and your children as well as any problems.' Parenting Research Centre

Kids love their parents to be united. However much they may push against it or try to divide them, they like the firmness of this boundary because it makes them feel doubly safe, and because they like to know their parents are interconnected and cohesive. It also, as parents, feels very good to know you consult each other on parenting issues, make decisions together and are strong on backing each other up too. I remember moaning to my dad because he and mum had thwarted something I was keen to do, and him saying: 'Until you're old enough, we often have to decide what's best for you. We do it together and we try to get it right. Sometimes we won't. But we do our best.' It had a big impact on me. Suddenly I saw them as two people who loved each other, loved me and my sister, and were united on doing just that – their very best for us. I also always liked knowing they didn't undermine each other. I wanted them to be a strong team, running our family – it made me feel safe, and proud of them.

Generations on, I see objectively how friends' children and grandchildren are just the same – when their parents are joint decision-makers and good, confident leaders, they are relaxed. Rebellious sometimes, for sure, but actually pleased to have a mum and dad who are united in parenting them. Having kids who feel secure with your parenting creates a great feeling in your relationship, as does the feeling of togetherness and mutual support it gives you. Conversely, if you don't back each other up it encourages the kids to manipulate one or both of you, and ends up in their secretly wishing you would be a strong partnership for them to look up to.

Family discussions are great: they create a feeling of involvement and self-esteem for each member. But ultimately the parents are the leaders so togetherness is crucial. Two heads, as well, are better than one at finding wisdom and the best answers, solutions and ways forward.

Two minds working together and supporting each other within the family unit also draw you close in body, heart and soul. It's a giver of happiness.

BRING THE CHILDREN INTO DOMESTIC QUESTIONS AND DECISIONS

Children love to feel involved in discussions and they are as much members of the household as you and your partner, so involve them in occasional or regular meetings to discuss household matters.

They will take as much interest as they wish and are able to for their respective age groups. Have some basic ground rules – everyone listens to whoever is speaking and on no account rubbishes what anyone else says; each takes it in turn to have their say, no one hogs the limelight; if anyone isn't interested or can't be serious when everyone else wants to be, they can leave the 'meeting'. You and your partner are the group leaders and make sure the rules are respected. It can be as often as decisions need to be made or for a regular taking stock – for instance once a week. Obviously, don't discuss your finances or anything else that might worry the children. This is just about general family matters that everyone can relate to. Being the leaders draws you close, and being included – with you both at the helm – makes the kids feel honoured, valued, appreciated and loved and in turn increases all these in their opinion of you.

BE INVOLVED IN PARENTING IN YOUR OWN WAY

Stay involved as parents, even if one or other of you does the lion's share of the practical aspects. Be as flexible as possible. It gives a great sense of security to kids if they know you can both shoulder the various tasks of parenting, for instance cooking. It's also good, though, to share parenting by knowing the aspects you're each best at or particularly enjoy. The important thing is to be happy with the way you share parenting so that neither feels overloaded or put upon.

As well as the family talks mentioned above, have regular catch-up discussions on your own, taking in what's going on with your kids just now and how you're getting along on the parenting front. Inspire each other to continue being great parents. It can help to remember what it felt like to be a kid. How can you, as their parents, make the experience a great one for your children? Think it through and action it and share their pleasure and fulfilment.

IN ALL THE UPS AND DOWNS OF FAMILY LIFE, REMEMBER THAT LOVE AND JOY ARE AT ITS HEART

After enjoying pleasing yourselves as adults, it can come as quite a shock to suddenly find your lives pretty much taken over by a new-born baby, and to realize that the commitment will continue to be intensive for the next 20 or so years and to some degree lifelong! The greatest key of all to being happy parents – and thus allowing happiness to continue in your relationship too – is to remember that love and joy are an intrinsic part of it – in fact the heart of it. Can you forget? Certainly – many parents get so weighed down with problems that they lose sight of the reasons for having children and the bliss of it, and feel trapped instead. It's natural to occasionally regret the loss of your old freedom, so don't feel guilty – the key is to acknowledge it and gently but firmly remind yourself that most ways of life have pros and cons, but you can always choose to major on the positives. Remember that whenever regrets or worries crop up, such thoughts are natural but you have two choices – wallow in gloom or choose to remember the wonderful and good things about having kids. Children are great joy-givers and parenting is in myriad ways hugely rewarding. Above all, having children is a world of love. The moment you reflect on this, the negativity will evaporate. Learn more about choosing a positive attitude and how it transforms all aspects of life in Secret 29 – Positivity pays dividends.

Putting it all together

Being parents is unquestionably hugely challenging but can be an immensely rewarding way of life that enriches your relationship with a unique and very deep kind of happiness. The great Secret of parenthood adding pleasure and fulfilment to your togetherness is to see it throughout the years as a joint enterprise that you are equally committed to and prepared to undertake positively, willingly and above all with a sense of joy and a remembrance, always, of the flow of love between you all.

All families have ups and downs. Rise to the problems in the same spirit as you spontaneously enjoy the good times – positively and willingly and with the bond between you as parents and lovers strong and sure. Then you can come through your relationship as a couple strengthened and with your happiness together glowing brightly. Being parents is a very special kind of togetherness – enjoy it, together.

24 Take time to be yourselves

> 'Your time is limited, so don't waste it living someone else's life.'
> Steve Jobs

> 'Despite the benefits, there is danger in constant relationship. We are wise to consider what they may be. And we neglect time alone at our own peril.' Joshua Becker

> 'Having time without your significant other glued to your side allows you to keep on track with the other things that make you happy and feel fulfilled.' Jen Kirsch

> 'Time alone also gives partners time to process their thoughts, pursue hobbies and relax without responsibilities to others.'
> Dr Terri L. Orbuch

> 'Having time apart is extremely healthy and keeps a freshness in their relationship. It encourages each person to maintain their own sense of identity while still being a couple, and it fosters independence and strength rather than neediness and clinginess.' John Aiken

We all need time with others without our partner around, and also some solitude. It gives you the chance to remember your identity and your purpose in life. However much you relish each other's company, it will soak you up if it's 24/7. Even if your partner is the nicest person in the world, who wouldn't ever dream of trying to take you over, they will probably try to influence you – and you them. And even if they don't, if you're with them most of the time you're bound to be heavily influenced by them and vice versa.

So you both need space and it's a compliment to your partner too. It's a bit of a balancing act because you don't want to cloister yourself away too much or you might find yourselves in a habit of not spending enough time together. It's some and some.

And a big part of the Secret is that time together becomes especially enjoyable when interspersed with time apart. You each need goods and hobbies of your own. It brings interest and spice to your relationship. It also revitalizes your spirit. You're not clones of each other, and tempting as it can be in the early stages to think you're incredibly alike, it's good to remember that despite similarities you are also different from each other. You are two unique personalities with two sets of abilities, talents, likes and tastes. You'll naturally gravitate, if you give yourselves the chance, to activities and interests that suit you, and doing so gives you the chance to freshen up your spirit and find new or renewed inspiration. This in turn brightens up your relationship.

Solitude and time with our own friends and pastimes is air for the soul. We need it. So never ever feel guilty about taking time for yourself. Encourage your partner to do the same and refuse to be coerced into an idea that you're so good together you don't need it. However much you love each other and enjoy being together, some time apart is invaluable to your relationship. With space to be yourselves, you'll come together refreshed and renewed.

ENJOY SOME 'YOU TIME'

Forget the idea that it's selfish to have some 'you time'. Space to be yourself isn't an indulgence – it's a necessity for your individual health and your relationship's. So carve some time each week and if possible each day to be alone or with others without your partner. Be conscious of the gift of this time to yourself and your relationship, so indirectly to your partner too because they will be encouraged to appreciate their own time as well. It won't happen without you choosing to make it happen, so schedule it into your diary and make it a priority to honour it.

That may also take some thought and planning. Think about what you'd really like to do with your time. Some solitude? That's fine. So is time with friends who lift you up in spirit and inspire you. Choosing voluntary work or visiting someone you know who would love to see you counts too (as long as it makes you feel good and doesn't depress you in which case it's not 'you time'). Or you may wish to rest, reading a book or magazine if that's a treat, or do something really active physically or mentally. We'll look at artist 'outings' too in the next paragraph. It's absolutely up to you. It's your time – decide what to do with it so that it doesn't just evaporate. Whether you choose to be alone or with others, appreciate each moment and feel it doing you good. All you have to do is take it gladly and use it, just for you.

UNLEASH YOUR INNER ARTIST

You're creative and multi-talented artistically – please don't protest – you are! And you need to cherish it and find outlets for your creative energy. It isn't necessarily about being an artist in any of the visual, musical or dramatic arts – your ability to be creative can show up in all aspects of life in the way you think and live. So use the time you put aside for yourself to let your creativity come through to the forefront of your mind. You might like to meditate, sitting quietly or while walking, letting your thoughts come and go and being aware of any fresh ideas or feelings you have. Or do something expressly to nourish your creativity – for instance, visiting an art exhibition or the theatre. Go with a friend if you wish, but do remember that it's fine to go alone – in fact it can be highly rewarding to be on your own with no one else to think about. Having this creative time just for yourself will feed into your relationship in all kinds of good ways, invigorating your love and interest in each other and enriching your togetherness just as it's enriched your spirit and perception of the world.

BRING THE ENERGY AND LIGHT-HEARTEDNESS TO YOUR RELATIONSHIP

When you're with your partner again, after your time apart, let the happiness and inspiration you've experienced flow into your togetherness. Show vividly that while you had a good time it's lovely to see them again. They will notice how much you evidently enjoyed yourself but above all how you bring this happiness back into your togetherness. That way they'll see how therapeutic it is for you and be glad it reflects lots of light and energy into your life as a couple too. It will also encourage them to enjoy their own space, making them much more pleasurable to live with too. Take an active interest in each other's interests but don't pry or push them to talk about it if they'd rather not. Encourage each other to replenish your individual spirit in your own space and in a way hug each other with your good feelings when you're back together again.

Putting it all together

Having some time to yourself is hugely beneficial, not just to your own wellbeing but your relationship's too. If your partner doesn't understand why you need some time to yourself, it may be because they feel possessive. Explain gently but firmly that you enjoy having space and that because it in a sense shines and feeds your spirit it will be good for your togetherness too as you'll come together again replenished and personally content. Personal contentment and inspiration is something we enable and give to ourselves – no one else, not even the most loved partner in the world, can be everything to us. Happiness begins within and then flows through the relationship. It's all about balance. Have plenty of space alone, and lots of togetherness – the two complement each other and will keep your relationship synchronizing beautifully.

25 Forgive

> 'There's no reason why we can't disagree whilst still being agreeable.' Barack Obama

> 'The weak can never forgive. Forgiveness is the attribute of the strong.' Mohandas Gandhi

> 'When you forgive, you in no way change the past – but you sure do change the future.' Bernard Meltzer

> 'There is no love without forgiveness, and there is no forgiveness without love.' Bryant H. McGill

> 'How do you know if you have forgiven? You tend to have nothing left to say about it all.' Clarissa Pinkola Estés

Forgiving is a healing balm in relationships and a must for happiness because it clears disagreeability. For how can you feel happy when you're seething about something your partner's done, and how can you be happy knowing they're mad at you? It needn't be a current issue that's riling one or both of you – it can be something deep in the past and even ostensibly buried. Anything that's caused rancour is going to affect the present and the best way – indeed the only way – to prevent it from causing ongoing unsettlement is to decide to be forgiving and then do it.

Forgiveness is incredibly healing, and the process of healing is helped hugely by forgiving.

Please don't panic and think: 'But I can't forgive him/her.' We can all be forgiving somehow, somewhere in the whole spectrum of forgiveness. You might not need to say and feel 'I forgive' as such – but there are many forms of forgiveness and we'll look at some of them. Mostly it's about deciding to shed the bitterness before it derails your own peace and your relationship. People think it's hugely complicated. Certainly the issues of hurt may be complex, but forgiving is a simple act of consciously letting go of the negative emotions and replacing them with a positive mindset.

You are already very positive in that you are choosing to be with your partner and you want your relationship to be happy and a lovely place to be. That's a great base for a forgiving togetherness. Forgiveness wipes clean any dross of blame and shame existing or lingering between you, enabling the happiness you seek. It also feels personally fantastic to forgive – truly like a weight off your shoulders. And it's immensely good, too, when your partner lets go of niggling memories about certain behaviours or incidents that have upset them. Suddenly you're both in the clear, unfettered by grudges and fear. Fear? Yes, for when we are blaming each other for something it's usually a sign we are harbouring anger at being treated badly or thoughtlessly. We're scared they will do it again and use bitterness as a form of passive resistance. Living forgivingly means letting down this defence but it does not mean being a pushover or weak. It's a sign of strength and self-respect that attracts reciprocal respect. And as well as doing good, forgiving always feels good in itself.

DECIDE TO LIVE FORGIVINGLY AND BEGIN PRACTISING NOW

Try saying it now: 'I'm going to be forgiving.' Imagine all hurt and residual bitterness falling from you and disappearing. Feel how your body is reacting. As I write this, I'm doing exactly this – reminding myself to be forgiving. I feel myself breathing deeply and exhaling pent up negativity. You too will probably feel your shoulders relaxing. Stretch out your spine and neck and feel the relief, mind, body and soul. When we're bitter about someone's behaviour, it tenses us up and makes us uncomfortable physically as well as emotionally. Don't worry that the anger pops up again. Negative feelings do recur but you're in charge of them now. So simply register any acrimonious feeling, remember you're living forgivingly and let it go again.

REMEMBER HOW MUCH YOU LOVE YOUR PARTNER

Another way is to replace it with a positive thought about your partner and think how much you love him. It's the opposite of being vindictive. If you're claiming 'I'm not vindictive', then think again. To not forgive is to be agnostic towards your partner. To believe you are hiding this is a delusion. Vindictiveness goes hand in hand with accusatory thoughts and even if you keep silent about them it's still aggressive. Ditch it – it's the only way. If your partner keeps repeating the hurtful behaviour, stop the cycle from repeating itself by stating how you feel when they do it and discussing a viable solution that is positive whether it involves acceptance or change on the part of either or both of you. Then step into the future positively and agreeably, and determinedly don't revisit past hurt. Remember that living forgivingly is a sign of positivity and strong character and feel the strength and mutual respect that living forgivingly brings. Forgiving helps you to stand firm against any kind of hurt or abuse and to expect and attract respectful behaviour that reflects your love for each other.

DEAL SENSIBLY AND CONSTRUCTIVELY WITH GRIEVANCES, THEN LEAVE THEM BEHIND YOU

Whatever the grievance was, leave it where it belongs – in the past. It can help to imagine yourself putting it in a filing cabinet labelled 'Done and Dusted – Don't Go There Again' or better still put it through the shredder. And don't go there. Refuse to entertain thoughts about it and absolutely don't allow yourself to obsess about it ever again. As above, dismiss thoughts about it immediately they involuntarily resurface. Sense the feeling of freedom and positivity this opens up. It's like letting light and fresh air into your mind and your relationship because without bitterness and ongoing acrimoniousness you are free in spirit and can love each other wholeheartedly.

Life and love are easier when you live forgivingly.

Putting it all together

Forgiving is a benediction for both of you and an essential Secret for your happiness together. It's not about patronizingly telling your partner you forgive them or in any way being martyr-like. It's straightforwardly deciding to let go of negative feelings and intentions about a perceived misdemeanour and not going there again. It gives you a fantastic feeling of relief and freedom when you shed the tension of bitterness and recrimination. When you both live forgivingly like this it's like a healing balm that gives your whole relationship a chance to start afresh unfettered by recurring accusations and doubts. Love can flow between you with no snags to block its way. It's also good for your relationship because any disagreements that arise can be resolved so much more easily when you're not confusing them with past issues and bringing those negative emotions into the current conflict.

It's a common misperception that we have to forget to forgive. Please don't feel you can't forgive because there's no way you can forget – the two aren't linked. Your brain will automatically bring up memories of any hurts you've received; so you can't forget at will, only time can fade a memory. But you can help yourself forget, in due course, by refusing to allow recurring memories of any hurt to settle in your thoughts, refusing even more determinedly to obsess about them, dismissing any wish to blame and shame your partner, and replacing them all with positive thoughts about them and your love for each other.

Bring love into your relationship actively any time and every day and you are automatically living forgivingly because the two are inextricably linked. With love you don't just leave negativity about previous behaviour in the past where it belongs, you invite each other to avoid hurting each other in the present and future. Forgiveness is loving and courteous and it attracts continuing considered courtesy and love. Love is the answer to most relationship issues. Love is forgiveness. Forgiveness is love.

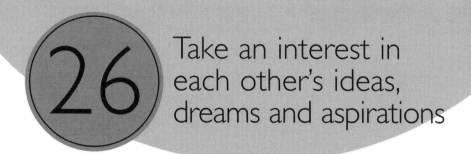

26 Take an interest in each other's ideas, dreams and aspirations

'Listening is a magnetic and strange thing, a creative force. The friends who listen to us are the ones we move toward. When we are listened to, it creates us, makes us unfold and expand.'
Karl A. Menninger

'The true secret of happiness lies in taking a genuine interest in all the details of daily life.' William Morris

'Develop interest in life as you see it; in people, things, literature, music – the world is so rich, simply throbbing with rich treasures, beautiful souls and interesting people. Forget yourself.' Henry Miller

'Any problem, big or small, within a family, always seems to start with bad communication. Someone isn't listening.' Emma Thompson

'When you are listening to somebody, completely, attentively, then you are listening not only to the words, but also to the feeling of what is being conveyed, to the whole of it, not part of it.' Jiddu Krishnamurti

Take a keen interest in each other's hopes, ambitions and thoughts on all kinds of aspects of life and you'll find it immensely stimulating. You'll learn a lot about your partner and keep abreast of how they develop as they mature. And the way you fascinated and inspired each other when you first met will constantly refresh itself and keep your love fresh and enjoyable too. It wakes you up mentally and reminds you what interesting people you are and how you love each other's vitality and zest for life. Your minds are the most precious assets you have and interlinking them in one-to-one, focused conversation keeps you flourishing intellectually and your relationship buzzing with mutual attention too.

It's really all about paying attention to each other. It's flattering and soothing, encouraging and motivating all at the same time. The more you know you're inspiring each other's interest, the more you'll each want to ensure you are interesting. Beware of not listening becoming a habit and even becoming bored with each other. Listen and learn, take a keen interest, share your dreams and thoughts too and all this will conspire to oust any tendency to be boring or bored.

It doesn't mean you have to lead exciting lives or be hugely intelligent. The simplest of us can be fascinating to be with if we think and look sideways at the world, ponder our thoughts and others, look positively at every viewpoint, every aspect. The more you listen to each other, the more you'll encourage this mind fertility. The more you listen to each other the more you'll kindle and rekindle over and over again that original spark between you.

Being positive is a crucial element of interest. If you disrespect everything each other says, the negativity will soak into the space between you, making you each loath to keep talking. Take a positive interest and help each other look positively at wishes and ways and possible outcomes – then you'll want to talk.

It's all about exploration leading around each other's mind. An ardent interest in your ideas opens up a field of gold – a rapport that will last you your lifetime together. Seize this energy, this inspiration and aspect of love every day of your life.

INSPIRE EACH OTHER TO HAVE IDEAS AND DREAM

Encourage each other to talk about their ideas, inspirations and ambitions. Lead the way in this by asking questions that will draw your partner out and show you are interested. For instance, simply: 'What do you think about so and so…' regarding an issue that's come up in the news or at work that's made you think.

Be genuinely curious about their thoughts. Once the question occurs to you, you won't have to pretend interest – you love them so you're going to want to know what they are thinking. Be careful not to respond with negative comments or even worse seem disinterested or apathetic. Show your interest with eye contact and expressions that show you're attentive.

It's the same with hopes and ambitions. Remember how fascinated you were with each other's when you first met? Reawaken this interest and be absorbed by the way your ideas bounce back and forth – giving you each a new take on the subject. Don't be riled if they don't at first return the compliment by asking about your ideas and hopes. Take your turn in talking about them as though they have asked but remember not to hog the limelight – bring them quickly back in. This kind of 'tennis' conversation – batting the communication ball back and forth between you – keeps the communication channels open and your love flowing. And tell them how you love to listen and talk with them – they won't know for sure unless you do! One of the greatest compliments and encouragements you can give your partner is to say 'I love talking to you!'

LISTEN TO EACH OTHER

The greatest compliment you can give is to truly listen. So take in what you hear, focus on it, think about it, ask questions to clarify anything you're unsure of. Again, you're drawing them out and all the time learning. Avoid the common trap of being so busy thinking of what you want to say you miss what they're saying. Good couple conversation isn't about standing on your soapbox pronouncing your opinions. It's about taking in each other's opinions, learning from them and mutually growing in understanding of each other so that your interest continues and is vibrant and fun.

Always respond thoughtfully, with care for their feelings. If you remember, too, what's been said, your mutual understanding of each other will continue to deepen and grow. Listening well is a true art and one that illuminates and brightens life and love.

APPRECIATE EACH OTHER'S SENSITIVITY
AND SENSIBILITY

Remember that when you share dreams and ambitions you hold your partner's soul in your hands, and they yours. Take the responsibility to care for this honour seriously – you may be the only person they've ever spoken to about it – by respecting their thoughts. It's hugely important not to deride anything they say, be negative or even tease. Take time to 'hold' the idea before you comment so you can take it in. Then say something positive. If you don't know what to say, something like 'Wow, what a thought – that's really interesting' will show you value them and their mind. Finishing any intimate conversations of this kind with 'It's so good to talk – I do love you' is reassuring and draws you even closer. Being each other's confidante is a simple way to give each other the happiness of your thoughts being listened to and valued. Of course it means you each feel valued too and that gives a rich glow of happiness. Show and speak your love in mutual interest.

Putting it all together

Taking an interest in each other's ideas, dreams and aspirations is stimulating and challenging, so you stay fully engaged with each other, mind to mind, spirit to soul. It shows you care, want to understand and, as you listen and share your own thoughts more and more, do understand each other. It keeps you in touch with where you both are in life now – not where you used to be but how you're changing and growing. So it helps you keep on parallel tracks, pacing yourselves to stay the course and enjoying every day of it.

We all need a confidante. Someone who is truly interested and willing to share their dreams too. Someone with whom we can bounce ideas back and forth, all the time learning a bit more about them and about each other, all the time inspiring and being inspired, comforting and being comforted. There is no greater compliment and honour you can give each other than listening with true interest, safe in the knowledge that whatever you say will be accepted and considered not just courteously, important though that is, but with a wish to be on side – there for each other to encourage individual thought and cherish your right to have it. You may or may not agree – that in a sense is irrelevant. The happiness factor is in the sharing, listening, respecting and love that flows between you. And the being interested. It makes you both feel interesting to each other, and that is one of the greatest secrets of love – and happiness.

27 | Believe

> 'How you think determines how you act. How you act in turn determines how others react to you.' David J. Schwartz

> 'Believe in love. Believe in magic. Believe in others. Believe in yourself. Believe in your dreams. If you don't, who will?'
> Jon Bon Jovi

> 'You need to believe in yourself and what you do. Be tenacious and genuine.' Christian Louboutin

> 'Believe in the importance of love, for it is the strength and beauty that brings music to our souls.' Anon

> 'The light of starry dreams can only be seen once we escape the blinding cities of disbelief.' Shawn Purvis

Belief fires potential and possibility into life. It's hugely powerful and never more so than in strengthening and energizing a relationship. Lose the belief in the strength of your love and it weakens. Renew your confidence with zest and it strengthens. Perhaps there is an energy at work that we don't as yet fully understand, or it may be that with belief our behaviour and body language changes, positively influencing our interaction with our partner? The thing is, it works. Couples who wholeheartedly believe they will stay together, and together keep strong in this belief as the years go by, are almost certain to do so.

This belief may be an intrinsic part of us, born and nurtured by growing up with parents whose happy relationship lasted or is set to last their whole lives long. But all is not lost if we didn't have that kind of example – in fact, if our parents stayed together unhappily or split up it can make us determined not to repeat history. Whatever your individual background, with a dedicated belief in the staying potential of love and happy togetherness you can make sure this is your story.

Believe in your happiness together and its continuity through the years and you'll consciously and subconsciously check impulses to be less than kind and loving. Unconsciously, too, your faith in each other's loyalty and permanence will generate a deep seam of contentment and security that's a solid base as you journey through all the phases and stages of life. You'll be happy to keep renewing your commitment to each other, pledging your love every day.

Belief is a choice you can make, not because you are frightened of separation and/or being single but because your love is real and your wish to pledge your love permanently is heartfelt. It means believing in yourselves – that you are both strong and capable, and love and choose to be with each other not from a position of weakness but a great inner strength. It means believing in love and togetherness not because it's what your parents did or didn't do, but because you implicitly know it's good and right for you as a couple. And because it's what – deeply, genuinely – you both want.

🧩 DON'T LET NEGATIVE OUTSIDE INFLUENCES INFILTRATE YOUR RELATIONSHIP

Remember your faith in the lasting power of love and happiness together. It's so easy to be influenced by the portrayal of marriage as a trap or disappointment – television dramas and films are full of disillusioned or downright nasty characters fighting and splitting up, and stars seem to fete their break-ups as badges of celebrity.

Stay in touch with the real world. It isn't cool to be spiteful to each other and always ready for a row. Love can and does endure when we believe in its essence – living our love every single day. Happiness too is about being loving and nice to each other, treating others, not just our partner, as we like to be treated. You know this is so. Believe in your love. Be loving.

Smile with the joy of it and be glad. You have the fundamental Secret in your heart and mind. Of course it takes two, so keep in close positive contact and communication with each other. Energize your love and happiness together with lots of affection and positive conversation. Nurture happiness with kindness and courtesy and by enjoying the small as well as the great pleasures of life together. Stay in touch with the real world of your relationship and make it loving.

BELIEVE IN EACH OTHER

We look at the power of trust in Secret 41. Also important to happiness is thinking well of each other. Seeing love, affection and pride in your partner's eyes, hearing them praise you, knowing they believe in you – your niceness, your many capabilities, your talents – feels fantastic. It boosts your self-confidence and puts bounce in your step. So do this for each other. Show your high regard not just in your eyes but in words. When they face a challenge, tell them you know they can do it. When they've done something or made something, tell them they're wonderful. Tell them you love them and are so proud and glad for them. Demonstrate your belief in each other. Praise each other's abilities and talents, boosting each other's self-confidence with your mutual positivity and support. Be glad your partner believes in you and show your appreciation by accepting compliments gracefully and joyfully and encourage them to do the same. Remember, they may seem like little things but they actually mean a lot. It feels so, so good to know your partner believes in you and it's one of the greatest gifts – and secrets of relationship happiness you can give each other. Accept their appreciation and belief in you unreservedly and be happy.

BELIEVE IN THE GIFT OF YOUR LOVE AND YOUR WISH TO STAY TOGETHER

Decide on happiness as your own and your relationship's default setting and help it stay firmly in place by refusing to dwell on worries about your relationship. Anxiety nags, unsettles and generally disturbs your peace and love, so refuse to waste time and happiness on it and absolutely don't fall into the habit of obsessing about it. Instead, make it your practice to face up to, confront and resolve any existing issues between you and any that come up. Help this process hugely by consciously remembering and believing in your mutual intention, agreement and ability to love steadfastly and joyfully. This last – to love each other joyfully – is so often forgotten. But love is all about joy. Take a step back if ever you're about to quarrel with each other and think positively. Remember the huge pleasure you found in loving each other when you first got together. Get this core of steadfastness and joy back into perspective in the centre of your love. It's like WD40 for a relationship and it's still there. Call it into being whenever you need to. Feel the joy of your love.

Putting it all together

Believe in the goodness and rightness of your relationship. It's your decision, your choice, and when you do you fly a flag of hope and courage and steadfast honour, calling you to love each other practically as well as emotionally every day as the years go by. Love and happiness are a leap of faith – every day – for a lasting relationship. They don't necessarily happen spontaneously – it's up to you to choose to believe in them and when you do you release a current of positivity and energy that makes loving and living positively not only a possibility but a certainty. Mutual belief in the love you share and in the happiness of being together feels wonderful and smooths out the wrinkles and upsets of daily life. It soothes ruffled feelings too, and gives you the incentive and ability to resolve any issues and problems that need to be addressed. When you believe, both of you, in your mutual wish for happy togetherness and love that lasts a lifetime too, something seemingly magical happens. You do stay together. You are happy. Life together is good and life generally is all the better for it too. Guard against fearfulness and worry with every fibre of your being. Firmly dissolve them when they are essentially unimportant or irrelevant. Confront and resolve them constructively when necessary. But above all replace negativity with positivity and belief in the goodness, rightness and happiness of your love. Let it flow between you, always – and enjoy.

28 Be compatible

'What counts in making a happy marriage is not so much how compatible you are but how you deal with incompatibility.' Leo Tolstoy

'A successful marriage requires falling in love many times, always with the same person.' Mignon McLaughlin

'Perfect is not when compatible people are together. It's when you're both opposites but in that way you complete each other.' Anon

'You don't suddenly become incompatible – it gradually develops if you don't care for your compatibility. So make sure you do take care.' Gwen Soane

'(Of her late husband and soulmate) We loved each other so we made sure we got on.' Lee Cousins

It's a frequent misperception that being compatible means sharing interests and taste and intrinsically having lots of other things in common too. Compatibility is certainly essential for mutual happiness in a relationship, but the wonderful Secret of it is that you can find it or create it even if you've precious little in common as individuals.

The essential knack is to work out how you can exist harmoniously for that is true compatibility. It's largely a matter of adaptability so that you learn how and then practise organizing yourselves so that you share your life together as the individuals you are but along parallel lines or interweaving your various thoughts, ideas and interests. You may or may not have the same or similar hobbies. Whatever they are they can still be complementary with mutual love, interest and thought. You may do a lot together or not much, but as long as you are interested in each other's interests and activities you'll be companionable.

You may share all the same friends or have your own sets of friends that rarely overlap – but as long as the two of you are a team, that's fine, you can still be in tune socially. Compatibility is about living with each other together – that is very much a part of each other's life and consciousness, loving each other always, working around each other, coming together often, keeping each other in mind when apart. It's a constantly adjusting partnership of two vibrant, fully charged people who choose and love to relate to each other.

So however similar or different the two of you are, from day to day find a way of life that suits you both. Always be happy for each other to grow – why wouldn't you be – and yet so often a couple will try to stifle each other's growth and vibrancy. Go the other way – encourage each other to develop, mature and reach for your own particular stars. Be comfortable together and then you can move in unison. Stretch your relationship and your togetherness to fit the way you are now. Do so willingly and happily and they will fall beautifully into place.

DELIGHT IN THE WAY YOU COMPLEMENT EACH OTHER

Remember that compatibility is your choice as a couple. Take your mind back to when you were first attracted to each other. You'd have been looking for all the ways you were compatible and flexibly adjusting to fit your personalities and lifestyles together. It was fun and a natural process. It still can be. The possibility of being compatible is there for you every day. It doesn't mean changing your personalities or stifling your individual taste and preferences. Rather, you're aware of your similarities and differences and delight in the way you offset and complement each other. Take an interest, too, in the way you both change over the years and be ready to change the way you interact and move through life alongside each other. Be accommodating as much as possible without compromising your character, and be super-understanding and sensitive to each other's needs and wishes.

SHAPE THE WAY YOU GET ON TOGETHER WITH ATTENTION AND LOVE

Be ready to adjust the dynamic of your relationship as suits you both best in any situation or phase of your life together. Be flexible in the various strands of your life Sometimes you'll be the leader, sometimes your partner will – but always be a team.

Think of being like two skaters or dancers and aim to move in harmony and rhythm. As you go through life together, read each other's minds and signals as much as you can and be very aware of each other, very much in unison. It doesn't just happen – it takes a lot of learning, a lot of adapting to each other's ways and it's very much energized and made possible by wanting to be good together. It's all about love. So remember you want to be together and can adapt your relationship as necessary to make it a delightful, comfortable place to be.

Keep your love for each other at the forefront of your minds and lives as you aim and plan, every single day, to get on well and enjoy living together. Love, love, love.

THINK SOLUTION NOT PROBLEM. THINK COMPATIBLE, NOT INCOMPATIBLE

Sometimes you may feel that you're nothing like when you met and don't fit together any more. Instead of thinking Problem! Think Solution! You know those wooden cube puzzles you get – take them apart and you couldn't imagine how all the angular pieces could possibly fit together? And yet with a little focus and practice and determination they do. The two of you will be like that sometimes – uncomfortable together or downright spikey even. With love, intention and attention you can work out how to place yourselves and your lives so that you fit together again. Think in terms of focusing on the things you do like about each other, not what you don't, and dovetail the differences in with your similarities. Look for the things you love about each other. Work out how to arrange schedules and interests and still find plenty of time for each other as you integrate your lives. Just as you choose to live together, choose to live together comfortably and smoothly.

Putting it all together

It's lovely to feel compatible. Life together is good. You fit together well. And that's exactly what happens – you fit yourselves together. It's not always, if ever, that you merge your interests, hobbies and tastes – rather you dovetail them because you wish and decide to. Remember that great example of when you first fell in love? You looked out for all the things you had in common and were entranced by the similarities. You hardly noticed any differences and those you spotted seemed interesting rather than making you think 'Oh no – we're not compatible'. You wanted to dovetail with each other, not just body, mind and soul but in all the practicalities of life together. And you did. It's actually no different now except that the decision to dovetail isn't an automatic one like then, it's something you choose over and over, just as you choose to love and support each other and to like each other. It's largely about remembering to fit and pull together rather than snagging against each other and pushing apart.

Look for the things you have in common and enjoy noticing more and more of them and, more and more, how good it feels to live alongside each other, a team that not only pulls together but loves doing so. Take care, always, of the way you get on, so you maintain your harmony, fully in tune with each other through the days and stages of your life together. Remember how important to you both your relationship is and how fundamental to your happiness. Cherish it for the intricate, amazing togetherness it is – two people so different in so many ways but together because you love the life you share, love yourselves, love each other. That's valid and vital, just as your ongoing interest in each other is. Be compatible – it's your choice – and appreciate it for the treasure on Earth it brings: the loving heartbeat of your happiness together and your whole relationship.

29 Positivity pays dividends

❝ *'Happiness is an attitude. We either make ourselves miserable, or happy and strong. The amount of work is the same.'*
Francesca Reigler

❝ *'There is little difference in people, but that little difference makes a big difference. The little difference is attitude. The big difference is whether it is positive or negative.'* W. Clement Stone

❝ *'You are never too old to set another goal or dream a new dream.'* C. S. Lewis

❝ *'Whatever you want to do, do it now. There are only so many tomorrows.'* Michael Landon

❝ *'Be soft. Do not let the world make you hard. Do not let pain make you hate. Do not let the bitterness steal your sweetness. Take pride that even though the rest of the world may disagree, you still believe it to be a beautiful place.'* Kurt Vonnegut

Except for those moments when bereavement, loss, illness or hormones suddenly strike, we always have two main choices of attitude – we can choose to think positively or negatively. It really is your choice whether you go into a positive or negative mode and the wonderful thing is that the more you choose the former the easier it gets until it becomes such a habit it's usually automatic. If positivity isn't your default setting, try it for a while. Consciously keep turning your thoughts and feelings around to a positive vibe. If that prospect bemuses you and you're already protesting 'But I feel totally negative so how on Earth can I be positive?' look at yourself, the situation and your place in it and think: 'OK, what would be the positive take on this? – there must be one – let's find it.'

A good way to start if your relationship is currently troubled, or you feel apathetic about it and your partner, is to literally make the best of it. That doesn't mean in any way taking second best. It's about looking at it in a different way, seeing all the positives. In so doing, you begin to create more and more of the best.

Your positivity will lighten the atmosphere not just around you but between you and in your home. It works in two ways of lightness. It shines light in so you can see the good and how to change the not-so-good aspects or at least positively adapt so they're happily liveable with for both of you. And it makes you feel lighter, so your spirits can soar again as they're meant to. When you carry negativity it's a huge burden that affects every aspect of you. It weighs you down. Without it, you'll have more energy, feel healthier, be better in everything you do. Positivity is not only weightless, it gives you energy that lifts you up. You can't carry your partner though – as with all the Secrets two people are involved. But your lightness will let your love for them, for yourself and for your life together radiate from you and encourage them to lighten up too. Positivity is love. Positivity is love in action, and it feels good.

LIST ALL THE POSITIVES

3

Start by making a list of the good things about your partner and ones you especially like. Now you – what do you like about yourself? You can't change your partner – but take care to let them know, often, there's so much you love about them – they'll bask in your appreciation and be encouraged to be and do their best. Same with you – appreciate yourself and welcome their love and appreciation too. Really feel your appreciation of all these good things in your life. Relish every iota of your good fortune and be and do your best. It's the positive way and it feels brilliant. It's not about delusion, lest you're cynically wondering. It's about maximizing all that's good and letting your 100% positivity bring it into every aspect of your life and especially your relationship.

BE POSITIVE IN ALL KINDS OF PRACTICAL WAYS

Enable and enrich your love with a positive attitude. At the same time, be very proactive too. Remember – no talking down your partner or your relationship with your friends and family, ever. Talk it up. And act positively to steer the dynamic between you. Positivity ousts needless and fruitless negativity. No more arguing, rowing or sulking. Talk to each other as though you love each other and want to be together – well you do, don't you? So be nice to each other, do some things together and positively, enthusiastically enjoy. Turn your relationship to the light – see the lovely colours and the good that exists and you'll automatically move it in the direction of its full potential. You may be saying: 'Well it's all very well but he won't change and we don't get on.' Again, take the positive realization. You're reading this book so either there's a lot of good about your relationship already to give you heart, or it's a last-ditch attempt to find a catalyst to improve it. Either way – you are the catalyst. Your becoming positive in thought, word and deed is almost certain to elicit a positive response in him because like attracts like. Lighten the way you interact. By letting this light show up all the good between you, you'll both feel the weightlessness and uplift of positivity instead of the burden of negativity.

But even if he's stuck in negativity and feels reluctant or currently unable to change, your positivity will revolutionize the way you think of him and your relationship and the way you are within and around it. Your demeanour will change – and positivity always feels good. Whether or not your partner joins you in thinking positively, remember you'll still be a catalyst for happiness. Recognize with your whole heart how good it feels to be positive.

RECOGNIZE THE MYTHS

Be aware of two false myths spread by cynics that perhaps your negative side will dwell on. They'll say positivity is burying your head in the sand. Absolutely not – in fact it's the opposite – it makes you constructive and productive. And they'll worry it will make you weak and even open you to being bullied. Again, definitely not. A positive attitude lifts your spirits up, boosts your health and strengthens you in mind too. It doesn't mean you'll be foolishly optimistic or short-sighted; It means you'll have high self-esteem and be confident in life generally and ready to be proactively and sensibly constructive.

Take great care to expect fairness, equality and proactive love in your relationship and accept nothing less. You'll be feisty and lively, fun to be with. Your partner may be curious at first and be ready to talk positivity through with them. Encourage them to take a positive attitude and way of life too. Above all, show in your behaviour and being how great a positive attitude is – not just for you but for your relationship too. Remember that a positive attitude gives self-esteem, confidence and strength. It enables you to expect, give out and accept nothing less than a fair, loving and equal relationship. Let your positivity shine and enjoy being lively and having fun together.

Putting it all together

Thinking positively has a beneficial effect on every aspect of our lives including our relationships and never more so than your prime relationship with your partner. It's a prerequisite for happiness, especially when someone else is involved. How can you be happy with them if you view them, or the way you relate to each other, negatively? Positivity recognizes and revels in all the good things about the two of you individually and together. In doing so, like a magnet it draws in more good feelings and love so you seem more attractive to each other emotionally, mentally and physically. Your relationship sparkles more in direct response. Positivity is an energy that revitalizes, lifts and inspires a positively active happiness. Depending on what else is going on in your lives, it could be the loveliness of being quietly peaceful together, each living your own life and dovetailing them seamlessly without having to think about it. Happiness purrs quietly and unobtrusively. Or it could, when you face troubles, be the inspiration and energy that sees you through and when possible enables you to constructively find solutions, adaptations and/or healing.

Positivity is mutual support through difficulties and life transitions. It's being there always, cheering each other up or on. It's a shared sense of humour, a positive interest in each other's thoughts, work and hobbies. It is love quietly appreciated, enjoyed and given thanks for. It hums with joy and/or contentment throughout your life together, harmonizing the way you individually are and your interaction. A positive attitude enables you to see all that's good between you and it gives you the ability, too, to nurture it so your happiness lasts a lifetime together. Contentedly. Joyously. Positively.

(30) Participate

> 'Such happiness as life is capable of comes from the full participation of all our powers in the endeavour to wrest from each changing situation of experience its own full and unique meaning.' John Dewey

> 'It's about experience, it's about participation, it is something more complex and more interesting than what is obvious.' Daniel Libeskind

> 'I alone cannot change the world, but I can cast a stone across the waters to create many ripples.' Mother Teresa

> 'You have to participate relentlessly in the manifestations of your own blessings. And once you have achieved a state of happiness, you must never become lax about maintaining it. You must make a mighty effort to keep swimming upward into that happiness forever, to stay afloat on top of it.' Elizabeth Gilbert

> 'The more connections you and your lover make, not just between your bodies, but between your minds, your hearts, and your souls, the more you will strengthen the fabric of your relationship, and the more real moments you will experience together.' Barbara De Angelis

After the excitement of your first months together it's easy to become complacent and soon find a kind of emotional and physical distance between you. And you're so busy with other things and people that demand your attention and full-on involvement. Then you suddenly realize, years on, that you've been sleepwalking through your relationship, never really registering with each other, never receiving or transmitting inner feelings, never doing much together, if at all. Detached instead of attached. The Secret of transforming this detachment is to participate fully again in your togetherness. That's what you got together for, wasn't it? To be together. To love each other. To do things together. To share not just your lives, important and lovely as that is, but your inner selves too.

In a way, it's a pretty monumental concept. We're so tuned in these days to the notion we're independent, individual, standalone beings – and of course we are all of those things – but the Secret of participating is that you can still be an independent individual while at the same time being fully with your partner, a team, sharing yourselves and this life together. Not as one, but as two wonderful, unique, loving people who just happen to love each other so much you chose to hook up together – and who continue to do so. How do I know all this? Because you're reading this. You've got a fundamentally good relationship or the makings of one, and you want to make sure it's truly happy – that means that both of you are happy, both committed, both participating fully. And participating feels not just right, in the circumstances of living together, but – well, I can't praise it highly enough – it feels fantastic.

Certainly, the act of taking part demands some effort – but it's not hard work – it's a pleasure. And once you've become practised at joining in together, engaging and sharing your renewed connection becomes second nature. When you both take your part like this it reawakens the kind of closeness you discovered at the beginning of your relationship. Feel the joy!

AS IDEAS COME TO YOU FOR DOING THINGS TOGETHER, PAY ATTENTION AND ACTION THEM

Every year you and your partner will have all kinds of ideas for things you could do together. Always, you have two choices: you can shelve them or action them. Don't be like so many and think later: 'Oh yes, we thought of doing so and so, but never got round to it.' Act on your ideas. Instead of letting them drop because you can't be bothered to research and action them, or forgetting because you didn't go that extra step. Focus on any good idea you have. Instead of pouring cold water on each other's ideas, be 'yes' people. Say 'Hey I like that idea. Let's do it!' Decide who's going to find out about it and then plan when, where and how you'll do it. Involve each other in the preparations and anticipation. Talk it up. Enjoy the thought. Follow it through by making any necessary booking or buying anything needed for it. So often I hear 'We keep meaning to xxx'. The road to total apathy is littered with things we meant to do and that would be sad for your relationship. Don't let it happen to your ideas. No more lost opportunities. Spring into action and do it!

Deciding to be 'yes' people is surprisingly easy, particularly when you encourage and support each other. Whichever of you has the idea, say 'Hey – that's a great idea. Let's do it!' Then agree who's organizing what and when and stay involved in the preparations even if your partner's in charge of a particular event. Enjoy the anticipation as well as the activity/event and delight in the way the shared pleasures bring you together.

PARTICIPATE TOGETHER AND JOIN TOGETHER ON THE HOME FRONT

You may have the common and sometimes justified fear that being too close might mean you'll be engulfed and lose yourself. But joining together isn't the same – your identity remains safe. You still keep your respective individuality and you can go it alone in a task as soon as either one wants to – there is no 'must' about it. But connecting in a shared pastime is great for togetherness and very satisfying. You tend to get more done, too. So make sure there are lots of times when you're both coming together in joining in.

It could be when there's a task to be done in the house or garden that will be quicker, easier, or just more enjoyable undertaken together. It could be doing the crossword or Sudoku together at coffee time instead of going it alone, or, if you like to do it on your own, you could photocopy it so you can both do it, side by side, for fun and for the invaluable mutual participation in the same thing. It's valuable because it means you join in, mind and body. You engage your brains on the same challenge and are close physically too. Enjoy the chemistry of it, revelling in the physical and emotional closeness as you pull together. Depending on what you're doing you stand to share laughter, thoughts, the sense of competing and/or pulling together in the same team. Feel how good it is and join together regularly and often.

PARTICIPATE FULLY, TOO, BY SHARING YOUR INNER SELF

Share your time, your thoughts, your oomph, your peacefulness. Take each other by the hand, for real and metaphorically. It's an expression of your wish to walk together through life. Your paths may diverge depending on work, hobbies, studies, family commitments, etc. but with a little thought and purpose you can still share with each other your joys and sorrows, thoughts and ideas. We're so used to putting up barriers to others to hide behind that it's easy to find yourself doing this with your partner too. Dismantle the barrier; you are an item and a team. Not only is it safe to share something of your inner selves with each other, as well as doing activities together, it's hugely beneficial to the way you relate overall. Sharing this way draws you close and reminds you why you're together – because you like each other and get on well and because you create a spark together.

Putting it all together

Take part in your relationship to the very best of your ability. There's nothing to lose and a rich seam of greatly fulfilling happiness to enjoy when you're fully involved, taking part practically, emotionally and physically. When the busyness of life has overtaken you and you've lost the habit of doing things together, you need to recognize it will take your full attention to pick it up again. Then it's only one easy step to doing just that – beginning to take part in your relationship in a fully involved spectrum of togetherness.

Sometimes we forget why we're together: it's because you want to be with each other. Not apart, not living together merely for convenience, but united to join in the whole process of living life to the full. It's an amazing, transcendent feeling to realize the potential. You are two people who love each other, want and choose to be together and can give each other an extra level of fulfilment and joy, whatever's happening in your life at the moment. You can do this just by participating in your togetherness and sharing your time and your selves actively and 100 per cent willingly. That sums it up – your 100 per cent willingness. Isn't that what it's all about? And every single particle of enthusiasm you add to the equation adds extra gloss and sparkle. Shine!

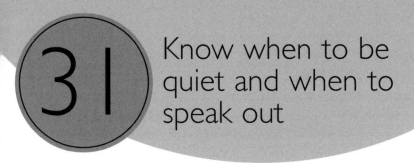

31 Know when to be quiet and when to speak out

> 'Words are the sea that you swim in, and while trying to be open and honest you have to be very careful.' Tim Lott

> 'It is only imperfection that complains of what is imperfect. The more perfect we are the more gentle and quiet we become towards the defects of others.' Joseph Addison

> 'Never for the sake of peace and quiet deny your convictions.' Dag Hammarskjöld

> 'It is common for thoughtless speech to stir up discord.' Dr Peter D. Kramer

> 'If you can't say something nice, don't say anything at all.' Anon

As we saw in Secret 3, I'm a huge advocate of positive communication in a relationship. It's the key to connecting with each other and helping mutual understanding. But sometimes we can overdo the talking and sometimes, too, it's better to say nothing at all.

The Secret of knowing whether it's best to say something at any time is to think of the 'com' in communication – that is, the 'together'. Ask yourself: 'Is what I'm about to say truly on the side of my partner, or is it really against them or at a tangent and/or purely pro-me?' – ask yourself, too, if it is going to help you both, working with you as a team?

If the answer to either of these questions is no, then keep quiet. It's as simple as that. Words used as weapons or that are likely to divide you are always harmful and best left unsaid. Words thrown out negatively when you're tired, hurt, angry, ill, hormonal or under the influence of alcohol or other substances are also potentially damaging.

Sensing when to keep quiet is an amalgamation of several Secrets: kindness, positivity, communication, sensitivity and being present in the moment and aware of the dynamic between you.

And yet it's so tempting to speak when we're feeling negative and it's also the time we're most likely to forget all the Secrets that usually guide us.

If you feel hurt, exhausted or dejected or in any other state of negativity and itching to take it out on your partner, it's a therapeutic strategy to go into another room or out for a walk. There you can lie low for a while and give yourself a chance to recover. Chances are then you'll be glad you didn't say anything and realize now it would have been negatively skewed. Similarly, if they are tired or stressed, leave them be to regain their equilibrium. Waiting until you are both in a balanced, positive state of mind is also eminently sensible if there's an issue between you that needs addressing. You can choose your words carefully then so they won't cause distress, or maybe see that there's no benefit in saying anything.

EXERCISE TACT

Tact is precious – it can save a lot of hurt feelings. It's great to have opinions and/or love talking, but always engage your brain first. It only takes a split second to do a rain check. What's the atmosphere like between you? Is your partner on good form or maybe a bit low? And you – are you in positive or negative mode? Get in the habit of watching what you're about to say and modifying it if you realize it could ruffle your partner's feelings or cause hurt. It can be fun to sound off and it can also release tension, but taking that moment to make sure you won't cause offence can save a lot of unnecessary conflict and/or hurt. The old saying, 'sticks and stones can hurt my bones but words can never hurt me', is clearly rubbish – words can be extremely hurtful. Use them with the greatest tact and care. Your love is precious – protect it with the Secret of knowing when to keep mum.

In any difference of opinion, two of the things guaranteed to annoy even the most placid of partners is crowing about it when you are proved right or not acknowledging you got something wrong. Far better to both live by Ogden Nash's maxim: 'Whenever you're wrong admit it and whenever you're right, keep quiet!'

RECOGNIZE THE VALUE OF A CUPPA

If your partner is feeling fractious and snappy and liable to throw verbal darts at you or encourage some from you, don't even attempt to talk to them other than greeting each other and other normal pleasantries like offering to make a cup of tea. And if they are clearly tetchy and likely to grouch at you, don't make yourself their target by staying close – move away, either physically into another room or by involving yourself in an activity. It gives them the chance to recover their equilibrium without any hurtful comments either way. This way you create a safe, quiet haven for them to chill out and get over the day's tension or perhaps a blood sugar low. In case of the latter, a couple of biscuits or other snack will be helpful without spoiling their appetite for their evening meal. It's just the same if it's you that's out of sorts or grumpy. A little peace and quiet and some refreshment works wonders. Now is definitely not the time for any exchange of words that might annoy or tire either one of you even more. You might, though, offer to be a supportive listener if and when they'd like to talk. Incidentally, the 'cuppa' we love so much and which is a useful metaphor for caring and comfort, is cited by many a happy couple as a brilliant ingredient in their happiness in its own right. Certainly it's about thoughtfulness for each other, but it's also an opportunity to share time and the enjoyment of a taste you like. Put the kettle on and brew up!

TAKE CARE TO LISTEN ATTENTIVELY AND THOUGHTFULLY

When you're talking it's vital to remember, and this applies to both of you of course, that listening is easily as important and often more so than pouring forth. If one of you hogs

133

the floor, the other will soon lose the will to try to join in the conversation. They'll probably stop listening too, or be so disgruntled by not having a chance to respond and share their thoughts that they'll snap, barging their way in and perhaps, in the stress of having to exert themselves, speaking much more negatively and less responsively and constructively as they would otherwise have done. So share the conversation and take turns to speak and listen. Repeat back what you think you've heard to make sure you've got it right, and then make an effort to understand without getting defensive. If you do feel attacked by something your partner's saying, though, don't lash back in self-defence and self-righteousness. They're not getting at you for the sake of it – they feel it needs saying so take it in and consider whether they've got a point. They should do the same for you if you're the one making a point. Remember, serious talk like this is a matter of clarifying thoughts and understanding, thinking logically and, mutually, adapting to each other fairly and lovingly so you get on well and happily. It's not a war – it's relationship diplomacy.

Putting it all together

So often we cause relationship problems because we speak out when we're in a bad mood and/or don't need to. Thoughtless pronouncements can cause offence, so beware sounding off spontaneously. It only takes a moment to pause and consider:

- Does this really need to be said?
- Will it or could it cause offence to your partner?
- If so, how can you word it to be as tactful, constructive, and kind as possible?

In any discussion, the key to keeping it positive, interesting and forward-going is to take turns talking and listening and in between reflecting on things to see if you're hearing right.

Your respective personalities are a big influence too in the 'to speak or not to speak' question. Knowing when it's a good idea to speak or keep quiet is often a matter of mutual understanding. Some of us are naturally more vocal than others and recognizing the difference between you and your partner is a great guide. Retreating to quietness and perhaps a little solitude can be all it takes to soothe tiredness at the end of the day and get you back into positive mode if negativity has threatened or overtaken one of you.

Awareness of the effect you'll have on your partner if you say something is all it takes to action your sense and sensibility. A moment's thought saves regret later and is a practical and easy aspect of love in action.

32 Manners and courtesy

❝ *'Good manners are appealing, alluring and sexy.'* Evelyn Resh

❝ *'Yes, it takes a bit of effort to be polite to your partner, but why would you want to treat your partner badly?'* Michelle Enis Vasquez

❝ *'It is a wise thing to be polite; consequently, it is a stupid thing to be rude.'* Arthur Schopenhauer

❝ *'Manners are a sensitive awareness of the feelings of others.'* Emily Post

❝ *'Allow both passion and courtesy into your life in equal measure, and be complete.'* Vera Nazarian

Good manners are a wonderful source of mutual happiness because they signal you still love and care for and find each other attractive. Yet while we're unfailingly polite, courteous and caring towards our friends and even strangers, it's easy to frequently forget our manners when it comes to our partner – and you often hear people being quite rude and even nasty to the person they love most in the world. Over-familiarity is probably the reason, and it's sad and indeed dangerous for a relationship, because we thrive on good care and kindness of which good manners and all manner of little (and large) courtesies are a vital ingredient.

A salient reminder of how important they are is to remember your first meetings. If one of you had behaved badly there wouldn't have been another date would there? And when you became an item, you almost certainly were still very careful with each other. When you settled down together you couldn't imagine ever not cherishing each other. You were gracious and loving pretty much all the time.

Early love is like this – good manners are the norm. So the first time we're confronted with our partner's sheer thoughtlessness, or at worst direct rudeness, it's quite a slap in the face. Sadly it can quickly become the norm of the relationship and as it does love starts to sour or simply fade.

Good manners go hand in hand with showing how much we care for each other's feelings and they are a vital Secret of happiness between you. Without them, an assumption soon pervades your relationship – for if your partner, who is supposed to love you most in the world, is careless of your feelings, you assume they care for you less than they once did.

Rudeness, on the other hand, is a downward spiral towards disconnection.

Courtesy encourages ongoing love and connection. It's thoughtful and tender and a way of showering each other with understated genuine affection. It makes life sweet and enables romance to keep flourishing. Maintain it steadfastly!

CHERISH YOUR IMPORTANCE TO EACH OTHER

Always remember and be glad that you are the key figures in each other's lives. You choose to be together and love each other and you are continually renewing this choice every day of your life. It's very important – probably the greatest life choice you will ever make. So value each other and show you do with politeness and courtesy. It's very largely about not taking each other for granted. Don't ever think: 'I can do whatever I like – they will love me anyway.' There is no guarantee of unconditional love and even the most adoring of partners may find their love dented and damaged by rudeness. Instead, appreciate and encourage your partner's ongoing love by showing you think well of them.

Remember at all times that love is nearly always conditional to some extent. It can withstand all kinds of tragedies, illnesses, accidents and disabilities, but if we're neglectful of common kindness and loving care of each other's feelings and wellbeing we sabotage it at our peril. Unquestionably, constant rudeness gets you down. It doesn't feel good to dish out or receive – in fact, it's likely to make you both miserable. So simply give up any rudeness, from open insults (even if said jokingly they can still wound) to more subtle undermining of confidence, and including personal traits that show you're no longer bothered about pleasing them. Replace these put-downs with thoughtfulness and respect for each other and yourselves. Don't insult each other, even in jest. Instead, boost each other's confidence in all kinds of ways. Respect each other genuinely and show it generously. Enjoy – it feels so, so much better.

MAINTAIN HIGH PERSONAL STANDARDS

Guard against a slipping of personal standards as this, too, displays a blatant disregard for your partner's feelings. Again in the early years together we're ultra-careful to behave as well as we know how to, for instance with good table manners and being discreet about bodily tendencies like, for instance belching loudly. Too often when a couple have been together a while they start forgetting to respect each other's feelings, even flaunting their less-than-savoury indiscretions. While familiarity is inevitable and can be lovely, don't overdo it in this regard. Far better to maintain or introduce a degree of reverence into your relationship by being, for your partner's benefit and because it actually feels so much nicer for ourselves too, good mannered and as fragrant and attractive in our personal habits and appearance as possible. It's a compliment to them and to yourself too as it encourages an inner and outer loveliness in you both. It's also an important ingredient in romance. It's a simple way to care for yourselves and each other and counts a lot in the happiness stakes. Make a pact and live respectfully and carefully with each other.

MAKE EACH OTHER COMFORTABLE BY BEING WELL MANNERED

Good manners have a common result – they make the other person feel comfortable. It also has a mirror effect in making you feel comfortable too. Courtesy is well documented in history and courtly love and general behaviour is perhaps where the theory and practice of etiquette began. Don't be misled by someone scoffing that good manners are precious or silly. They are a way of looking out for others' comfort and ease in a social setting and one's own. But it's true there's no need for over-complicated, unnecessary rituals that have become class-based. A simple way to be considerate is to do as you would be done by and speak as you'd prefer to be spoken to. An air of disapproval, unfailingly negative responses and unkindness in any other form from your partner can all get you down.

So, both of you, need to be positively encouraging to each other. Even when you can't agree, respect each other's right to their own opinion. Look for things you like to praise, do all you can to make them feel good about themselves and to realize their potential. Don't discourage them with thoughtless bad manners – encourage them with courtesy and you'll lift their spirits. You'll lift your happiness together too. Always remember the point of good manners – they make you both feel comfortable and it honestly feels far, far nicer than behaving badly. Even in disagreement, you can still be polite and in that ongoing atmosphere of courtesy, disputes are more easily resolved and agreement happily restored.

Putting it all together

Good manners and courtesy cost nothing yet are more valuable to your relationship and personal confidence than any material treasures. Maintain them diligently or reintroduce them if they've slipped because they are a key element of ongoing happiness together. When you treat each other with care and courtesy it feels comfortable and is a constant reminder that you mean a lot to each other. It's good for the one who's treated well and the one who's being well-mannered. Rudeness, on the other hand, is always unnecessary and never feels good either to the one who's behaving ignorantly or the recipient.

It's a common misconception that you don't have to bother to be polite to each other once you're settled into your relationship. And of course a good relationship can normally weather an occasional lapse from one or other of you and even find it funny or touching. But if your relationship or one of you happens to feel a bit fraught, you're tired or just need your partner to be there for you, lovingly supporting you (and who doesn't?) rudeness or thoughtlessness on the manners front can be hurtful. When counselling I've seen far too many people cry when they tell me the unkind or downright rude things their partner has said. I've seen a lot of confusion and/ or anger about bad manners, too. It's easy to think it doesn't matter to call your partner an idiot, for instance, or to say something negative about their appearance, or to neglect your own personal appearance, but all can be sensed by them as a kind of contempt for their feelings.

So take care not to dish out insults, even in jest; never ever be unkind about each other's appearance, and take care that you look after yourself and don't let your personal standards slip. Tenderness and general good behaviour in your relationship signify respect for each other. Make them your standard way of being and living and take care not to let your standards slip. They are a way of showing a kind of reverence for each other that is oxygen for romance.

Know each other's body clock (and other personal mood makers)

> 'There are things I can't force. I must adjust. There are times when the greatest change needed is a change of my viewpoint.' Denis Diderot

> 'We cannot direct the wind, but we can adjust the sails.' Dolly Parton

> 'I always try to adjust to the situation.' Novak Djokovic

> 'Life is the continuous adjustment of internal relations to external relations.' Herbert Spencer

> 'Finding out how you can work around the things you don't see eye to eye on is how relationships are cemented and are made to last.' Michael J. Henderson

We all have a personal set of natural inner rhythms that affect our moods, energy levels and feelings of wellbeing. The best-known one is usually called our body clock. We tend to fall into two categories: some of us are morning people, some of us are night people. You probably already know well which you and your partner are. If a night person you'll be most alert and active towards the end of the day and during the evening and even wide awake deep into the night. If you're a morning person the reverse is true – you're full of energy in the morning and start to fade in the evening, wanting to sleep at night. It's easy to do things together if you've similar 'clocks' but even so it's as well to be aware how much better you feel if you respect them.

Younger people, especially, may try to live up to friends' expectations of, for instance, staying out late, or getting up early, and end up grouchy and tired. Reminding each other that it's ok to follow your natural rhythms is really helpful. But even if you differ and are out of kilter, one a night owl, one a morning lark, you can avoid problems by being sympathetic to your respective daily cycles, working around them willingly and finding common times when you both feel upbeat and alert and can synchronize activity, and respecting each other's need to rest at their preferred times, too.

Sometimes, too, it's a case of compromising. One of the most frequent causes of sexual disharmony is when one wants to make love in the evening and the other longs only to veg out on the sofa or go to bed and sleep, or when one feels sexy first thing in the morning when they wake up and the other hates being woken or is too bleary eyed for the first hours of the day to even think about making love. Next, we'll look at how to remedy this comfortably for both of you.

There are also the natural swings in blood sugar levels and/ or temperament that affect most of us. Again, they don't have to cause disharmony – even if you can't empathize, you can sympathize and, in mutual understanding, support each other through them, getting on just fine despite your differences.

KNOW AND SYNCHRONIZE YOUR BODY CLOCKS

Agree it's good to spend some quality time together when neither of you is too sleepy to talk or take an active interest in something together and pinpoint times during your leisure hours when you can both be wide awake.

Plan a time conducive to mutually enjoying some active togetherness and make the most of it. For those of us who doze after our evening meal, it can be good, for instance, either to eat later so you have more 'up' time together beforehand, or instead of collapsing on the sofa, do something like going for a walk or playing a game that demands attention and engagement. If you both share the same body clock, go with its natural flow as much as possible and don't try to be something you're not. It feels good to be active at the best times for you. Of course it's fine to sometimes reverse your clock and do something like dancing most of the night when usually you're tucked up in bed!

You'll enjoy your natural rhythms all the more afterwards and the shared satisfaction and pleasure of synchronizing your lives around them so that you regularly share active times together and keep your interaction vibrant, engaged and interesting.

AGREE GOOD TIMES TO MAKE LOVE

Determine not to let differing body clocks scupper your sex life. Work around them and, as above, agree a time when you both can let yourselves go and wholeheartedly enjoy making love. It's important to be willing and up for it – good lovemaking is largely about being enthusiastic. We've seen before that sex is one of those things that, like playing a musical instrument, we may inexplicably shy away from practising, even though we know we'll love it once we get going. But mutually enjoyed sex is a Secret of relationship happiness all on its own (see Secrets 43 and 44). If desire isn't spontaneous, recall it from a time when it was; imagine it happening again now and let the feelings engulf you. In lovemaking, we are what we think and what we feel and both are in our control. So if you want to feel attracted to your partner and to enjoy making love, imagine the feeling, feel it to the full, and let it come into being for real in your relationship. Then just go for it, putting in a previously agreed amount of time, albeit approximate, so that you're neither too rushed for mutual fulfilment nor liable to think it's going on too long!

Too prescriptive? Well yes – but happiness in a relationship is largely prescribed – it's up to you to choose, invite and enjoy it and this is especially so in lovemaking. Feel arousal to the full and you enable yourself to start having a lovely time. Step on to the arousal curve and you release the feelgood hormones. Appreciate it all. It's a little bit of magic – actually it's a lot of magic – and all you have to do is synchronize your body clocks, set the time aside and think, 'Yes'!

UNDERSTAND THE NATURAL RHYTHMS OF YOUR BODIES AND MINDS

Learn your partner's other natural rhythms so when their blood sugar levels naturally dip or peak you're ready to give them a hug, conversation or some space for a quiet interlude. (See Secret 31.)

Use all your intuition and sympathy. We all have our own ways of dealing with our daily ups and downs and that's fine, but sometimes doing the opposite of your natural inclination can be helpful. For instance, I know that around 5 o'clock I'll suddenly feel exhausted. There are two ways of dealing with it to get my mojo back for the rest of the day. I can give up to it for half an hour or so, sitting down with a cup of tea and relaxing or, if I'm really busy, galvanizing myself into action and pushing through it. Help each other do what's right in the moment too. Being body clock and natural rhythm allies gives you a lovely feeling of mutual support and understanding.

Putting it all together

There'd be a lot fewer rows and ruffled feathers if we all learned to notice each other's natural mood swings throughout the day. Your partner thoughtfully thinking: 'Oh yes – she/he's tired around this time – I'll make a cuppa/suggest they have a break' can make a huge difference to how we cope with them without getting snappy. A little loving support helps us to bounce out of the mood quickly, too. Recognizing each other's body clocks also gives you a particularly nice feeling of empathy and of being in close accord. How good is it to be able to say 'He (or she) understands me so well – it's just lovely'? rather than that all-too-frequent refrain we hear: 'My partner doesn't understand me.'

Of course there are all sorts of other ways to understand each other, but daily mood swings happen to us all and recognizing and helping each other deal comfortably with them is a simple and rewarding thing for both of you. Not only are you pre-empting fractiousness and friction, you're averting a possible slide into a longer-lasting downtime. A cup of tea or a burst of physical activity are often all it takes to recover fast, regaining your mood and energy equilibrium. Served up by your partner, with lots of appropriate loving care and sympathy, and the feeling of restored wellbeing is even more rapid. It's simple to do, but an important factor in your mutual happiness.

34 Manage your finances

❝ *'The secret of a happy relationship? Talk to each other. Cut your cloth to your income. And enjoy it!'* Nick Jade

❝ *'Annual income twenty pounds, annual expenditure nineteen [pounds] nineteen [shillings] and six [pence], result happiness. Annual income twenty pounds, annual expenditure twenty pounds ought and six, result misery.'* Charles Dickens

❝ *'A little thought and a little kindness are often worth more than a great deal of money.'* John Ruskin

❝ *'Share joint expenses. Keep some individual money for your own spending but be prepared to help each other out.* Nick Lloyd

❝ *'The person who doesn't know where his next dollar is coming from usually doesn't know where his last dollar went.'* Anon

A balanced and agreed approach to your finances is an important feature of your happiness together.

You think money doesn't matter when you're first in love. You'll be happy, even if you didn't have a penny in the world, because your love is everything to you. And then… and then reality steps in. For money of course does matter. Not that we need wealth for relationship and general happiness. It's more what we don't need – a shortfall. As Dickens's Mr Micawber perceptively said, if our outgoings exceed our income we're going to be miserable. When worry unsettles you, anxiety pervades your relationship and your love, however strong, takes a battering.

All can still be well if you stand together, support each other and give each other hope, inspiration and practical help in resolving the situation. You don't need a lot, just enough.

So there are three things to remember at all costs (and yes, that's literally!). Discuss honestly and agree your financial strategy; in all contingencies, work forwards together – don't pull apart; and remember your fundamental love and ability to live together happily and harmoniously.

When you put your heads together to review your finances, resolve any issues or problems and budget accordingly, you have not just double but many times the ability and inspiration to do so comprehensively, realistically and powerfully. You are batting on the same side; no longer victims but the hero and heroine of this practical side of your life together.

Every couple has their own financial story and finds their own way to agree on and sort out a viable financial plan that works well and is conflict free. For there is no sensible need for conflict. Honesty and openness make for mutual understanding, which in turn enables that alchemical mixture of common sense and compromise to work its magic.

Because we're brought up, mostly, to keep our personal finances just that – intensely private, it takes a certain leap of faith to share our beliefs, ideas, foibles, failings and aspirations about money. Doing so takes a lot of trust and taking each other's thoughts and feelings on board takes a lot of love and consideration too. They reward you with a rich sense of togetherness, stress-free money management and the happiness that results.

AGREE TO DISCUSS FINANCES REGULARLY AND CHOOSE A GOOD TIME

Set aside a chunk of time when you want or need to discuss money matters. Pick a time conducive to maintaining a positive approach. Don't talk about finances when you are hungry or eating, and choose a body clock slot when you are both in a naturally good frame of mind (see Secret 33) so that your conversation won't be negatively skewed. Always agree the ground rules before you start talking.

First of all, remember to consciously dismiss emotion from your minds. Keep emotions out of it and be purely practical and constructive. Money is a practical consideration over which you are in control. Second, be totally open and honest with each other about your beliefs about money and habits. Dismiss any sense of shame or inadequacy. Yes, events like redundancy are distressing, but addressing them constructively gets you back in the driving seat. You are not victims, you are capable and can and will plan to deal with any situation in the best way possible. You are at the controls of your financial affairs. Third, seek experienced, expert advice whenever it will be helpful.

PLAN A MUTUALLY AGREEABLE BANKING ARRANGEMENT

Work out an arrangement that suits your personal ethos, your individual and combined income and your current situation. Be prepared to relax rigid attitudes to accommodate your points of view, and to compromise as you devise an arrangement that suits your coupledom. Be flexible both now, to accommodate your individual ideas, and so you can easily adjust to future circumstances.

Again, don't hesitate to seek advice if you'd like some help deciding what's best for you. Many couples find a combination of accounts is the best answer; each partner maintaining an individual one to retain their financial autonomy and also having a joint account into which they both contribute agreed amounts, depending on current incomes, to cover domestic and other shared expenses. As above, seek expert advice in exploring possibilities and finding the best arrangements for your particular relationship.

PLAN YOUR BUDGET AND STICK TO IT

Above all, budget sensibly. It puts you both in control of your current financial situation and will avoid future deficit. Some thought now, and regularly, will develop insight and understanding of the way finance works generally and the best way to harness it in your relationship. Having always worked and 'got by', I wish I'd had the advice years ago that I was relatively recently given and which I now pass on: 'Save a tenth of your income and budget to live on the remaining nine-tenths.' You can if you decide to, and it feels fantastic. Put your savings where they will give you a safe return and add this to the principal sum. It's exciting to watch this, as a couple, and see it mounting up as the interest compounds. For those who already do this, apologies – you already know the happiness it gives to not only be saving but saving as a couple. It draws you close, it inspires you to look after all areas of your finances, and it is remarkably generous in increasing self-esteem. Enjoy working out how to shape your expenditure to fit the 90 per cent lion's share of your income and enjoy, together, the tremendous satisfaction that this simple money management provides.

Putting it all together

It feels really good to devise and agree on the best way to arrange your finances together, and working together to implement and maintain your strategy. Once you're in harness to do this, you can adjust it through all life's stages and happenings and never again fight or feel disgruntled over differing habits. Having the courage to open up to each other develops the trust, love and consideration between you and they all work together as you apply your chosen formula. Successful money management, and in particular the joy of saving regularly and budgeting with the remainder of your income, adds another dimension of togetherness to your relationship.

Not fighting about money is perhaps the greatest enabler of happiness in any relationship. It has nothing to do with giving way or one of you putting up with any bad financial habits of the other. It's about working together to find the best way to organize the financial situation you share as a couple, to find solutions to any issues and problems as they arise, and to continue to work as a team in managing your money throughout your relationship.

Money is a tool for living, no more than that. It's not something to get emotional about; it's there to be used at your command the best way possible as the currency of your life. With good financial management and a shared approach to working together on your financial plan, you are free from the spectre of increasing debt to enjoy your relationship unencumbered by money worries. If you haven't already, start organizing your finances now, together as a couple. You'll be very pleasantly surprised how good it feels to be at the controls as a team and at how it makes for happiness between you.

35 Travel in the same direction

> 'Life has taught us that love does not consist of gazing at each other, but in looking together in the same direction.' Antoine de Saint-Exupéry

> 'I can't change the direction of the wind, but I can adjust my sails to always reach my destination.' Jimmy Dean

> 'Efforts and courage are not enough without purpose and direction.' John F. Kennedy

> 'It is the set of the sails, not the direction of the wind that determines which way we will go.' Jim Rohn

> 'If one advances confidently in the direction of his dreams, and endeavours to live the life which he has imagined, he will meet with a success unexpected in common hours.' Henry David Thoreau

Direction is an essential part of life. We can't stand still. We can't go backwards. Time – and every living thing – has movement and momentum. The only way is forward. If you want to be together, and enjoy all the potential happiness of togetherness (which is actually pretty immense, when you think about it), then it's clear you need to take the same direction. My sister, Dr Penny Stanway, who has been married to her husband Andrew for 40 years, says a together relationship is like you're following the same road together and practising football. You each have a ball of your own and sometimes one or other of you will go off-road looking for your ball, but soon you'll rejoin the other back on track.

Moving forwards through life, opting to keep on direction as a couple every day and repeatedly, again by choice, joining up again after every divergence, you follow the same path. It's a good way of life. This world, of course, can be enjoyed whether you are single or in a relationship, but having a soulmate beside you through the years is for many, and I hope and trust for you, a very special added blessing.

Like most good things, if you want to maintain them, it takes some energy and willpower. But that's no bad thing. Nowadays, it's so easy to separate. There's no longer, thankfully, a social stigma, and everyone knows couples who have broken up and thereafter move from relationship to relationship. An enduring happy relationship is becoming something of a rarity and in a way this makes it easier to stay together! When you are well aware of the occasional temptation to give up and go in separate directions, you are better placed to stay firm in your resolve to stay together. You can look more objectively at whatever's unsettled you and see it for what it is, a dispute or happening that actually doesn't have the power to break you up. You and your partner love each other, fundamentally, and see the whole picture of your happiness together. You stay on target – keeping your direction in togetherness, not just wishing but choosing to converge again and continue following your path through life as a couple. You love each other and follow love's momentum.

FEEL AND ENJOY THE ENERGY AND DIRECTION OF LIVING TOGETHER

Enjoy the momentum of living your lives together as a couple. Appreciate the energy that comes as you share direction and use it to the full, harnessing your potential to do more as a couple than you could on your own.

You each have boundless energy and so does love. It – and you – are powerful. Think in terms of harnessing your mutual energy by recognizing every day that you love each other, and being aware of being on the same path together. You are not stuck in your way of life, nor are you stuck together. Certainly, circumstances may look to be set for the next few years – perhaps for example in your careers, or because you are bringing up children, but they are still your choice and you choose to be there, together, on this particular stage of your life. Don't lose sight of the direction that you are pointing in. It is still there, always. Enjoy where you are to the full, for what it is, and enjoy the feeling of keeping pace with it and with each other, for the whole length of this phase.

PACE YOURSELVES TOGETHER

Throughout life, aim to stay in tandem so neither is pulling or pushing the other. Like running partners, you tacitly agree a speed and keep to it so that neither has a sense of being pulled backwards or forwards. Any journey, together, involves thought for each other. So look out, every step of the way, for each other's wellbeing, sharing your loads as much as possible and being prepared to relax or speed up to harmonize.

There may be times when one of you feels they're streets ahead of their partner in one segment of life (this is specifically addressed in the next Secret: Take your tiger to the mountain), but in general you progress through each day in tandem. Organize events and chores and pleasures as equally as possible so that neither is exhausted and feeling the other's not pulling their weight. You may need to relax a bit, do less and de-stress, or alternatively you may need to up your energy and do more. It's good to review how comfortably you're getting on as you follow the course of your life together. Take stock and adjust as necessary but, above all, appreciate the good things you share. Life is good. Feel it and enjoy your good fortune in loving each other and sharing the road with all your hearts.

SHARE YOUR EXPERIENCES AND IMPRESSIONS

Future, present and past, are all part of your journey as a couple. Together, enjoy the happy memories as well as looking forwards together. But, most of all, participate fully in the present and focus on being happy together right now.

Look forward to your life ahead together, enjoy good memories too and, above all, enjoy where you are right now. It's very important, wherever you are in life, to not be so busy getting things done and stretching forwards that you don't enjoy the all-round view of your life and your present patch. Ambition is fine too, but take care not to let it blind you to the pleasures of today. A sense of current time and place is what life is all about. So on your journey, be present and live in each moment, wherever you are in your life's path as individuals and as a couple together. Share your experiences and impressions. Keep pace with each other's maturing process too, and you'll help yourselves grow together.

Putting it all together

The feeling of united direction, whether the pace is slow or swift, is wonderfully emotive and draws you close. If you're fairly static at present because of circumstances, enjoy the feeling of treading water or floating in the relative stillness. Don't ever wish your time away – every moment of every day is precious. Hold hands actually and metaphorically. You're in this life together, by choice, and that's a wonderfully inspiring commitment. Mutual consideration is important whoever you are travelling with, but never more so than with your partner. Don't take each other for granted – appreciate their presence, their ideas, their personality, their physicality and encourage them to do the same for you. Love – and life – is the sweetest thing when you have someone who truly values you at and on your side.

A sense of direction is precious, too, in reminding you of the passage of time. You encourage each other to make the most of every day and every stage of life. Sometimes the pace of life is fast, sometimes slower, but always there are things along the way to enjoy – not least each other's presence. Advance confidently as you fulfil the dream of living happily together. A strong sense of direction, mutually chosen, followed and enjoyed, takes you along the path of and to your dreams. Move together gracefully and gratefully – thankful and serene in the knowledge that you are travelling companions through life and hugely fortunate to have found each other and to love, and to want to love, each other always. Enjoy this time in your journey, your memories and know that you will confidently face and cope with the challenges ahead. You are of your time.

36 Take your tiger to the mountain

'I've learned that waiting is the most difficult bit, and I want to get used to the feeling, knowing that you're with me, even when you're not by my side.' Paulo Coelho

'Patience is power. Patience is not an absence of action; rather it is "timing", it waits on the right time to act, for the right principles and in the right way.' Fulton J. Sheen

'"For a while" is a phrase whose length can't be measured. At least by the person who's waiting.' Haruki Murakami

'Will is of little importance, complaining is nothing, fame is nothing. Openness, patience, receptivity, solitude is everything.' Rainer Maria Rilke

'The strongest of all warriors are these two – Time and Patience.' Leo Tolstoy

There's a lot of interest today in personal development and there may be times when you feel you've become out of step with your partner because you've learned so much and in a way gone ahead of them on this front. Most couples find this happens occasionally and sometimes you can feel out of kilter for longer swathes of time. The 'Take your tiger to the mountain' philosophy is the illuminating Secret of maintaining both your personal happiness and your equilibrium as a couple when this happens.

It's a very useful metaphor to remind you of a strategy for dealing with it successfully, without holding back your progress, so that it doesn't come between you.

You imagine you take yourself – and your soul – to the slopes or top of a mountain. Your knowledge could be in a particular skill or it may just be that you've matured emotionally and in wisdom and your partner doesn't understand where you're coming from.

As you imagine you are sitting on the mountain, surrounded by beauty, stillness and the love of the whole universe stretching out all around, you wait, patiently, with great compassion in your heart for your partner in their own time and however long it takes to arrive at a similar place of maturity. For now you will be able to relate to each other comfortably as usual, and in time with mutual understanding.

Compassion is a huge part of this. It's very easy to get frustrated when your nearest and dearest doesn't understand a line of thought or the particular need you have at this point of your life. You might find yourself tempted to be scathing or more subtly patronizing, making them feel smaller than you and defensive and unhappy. But when you take your tiger – your inner spirit and wisdom – to the mountain you bear with them acceptingly and patiently as they grow at their own pace. You don't try to push them to speed up in their maturing or understanding, you don't – ever – and this is imperative – belittle or patronize them. You simply do your own thing in your particular stage of maturation, enjoying where you are to the full but neither expecting nor even encouraging them to hurry up and join you. You happily bide your time, knowing that whether or not they grow as you have is not part of your story. For you each have your own individual story and that's absolutely fine.

BE PATIENT

Remember the phrase 'Take your tiger to the mountain' whenever you feel frustrated that your partner is struggling to keep up with you in any respect. It could be, for example, that they behave or think immaturely, in your view, or can't understand your growing wisdom and maturation. The phrase is an instant reminder to bide your time happily as you imagine removing yourself from frustration and sitting on the mountainside, happily being you and letting your partner be their self too.

Remember, pressing others to mature may make them feel inadequate and suggest you are being demanding and patronizing. Be pleased about your own development and enjoy being you at this stage of your life. No one else can hold you back. No one can make you feel you somehow shouldn't be enjoying your progress in understanding. Enjoy it to the full, accept your partner's not on the same plane at the moment but perhaps will be in their own time and style. You're different and that's absolutely fine. Remember the gift of patience whenever you and/or your partner are frustrated by a differing style and speed of development in any sphere.

Decide to bide your time happily until and if they join you at your level of understanding. Meanwhile, be glad for your development and enjoy your wisdom.

EXPECT YOUR PARTNER'S UNDERSTANDING TOO

At the same time, it's important that they pay you the same respect you are showing them. Belittling, teasing designed to put you down or any other attempt to sabotage your learning and hold you back is not fair and unacceptable in any relationship, but completely off-limits in yours as you both love each other and are committed to mutual happiness together. Hopefully, they will understand that you are developing in your own way just as they are. It will be much easier for them to be accepting and uncritical when they realize that is just what you are and that you are not in any way trying to push or coerce them to emulate your individual progress. It's a kind of mutual magnanimousness – each of you respecting each other's current pace and place of development and accepting it benevolently. Be content you are each free to grow in your own way and enjoy your mutual acceptance and concord.

ENJOY THIS TIME OF LEARNING AND SELF-KNOWLEDGE

Appreciate the benefits of a waiting period. You are free to explore what you're doing and enjoy the level you're at or keep progressing in your own time. Enjoy, too, the feelings of love that mutual acceptance brings. Appreciate that although you're on different levels in this particular regard just now, you are nevertheless deeply committed to each other and to your mutual wellbeing. Be glad to share your enthusiasm and, if they show any interest in what you're doing, generously talk to them about it and show that you are happy to encourage them along the same path if they wish – but of course it's completely up to them and you're content either way. If they do join you, again resist any impulse to criticize their decision and their efforts. Be happy for them and for yourself in having their company and eschew any feeling of superiority! Remember your personal development is dependent only on you. While it's nice to have the participation or understanding of your partner, it's not a problem if you don't. Meanwhile, resist any opportunity to patronize them, remembering being on different learning curves doesn't make either of you more or less superior. Be glad you are together as a couple in all kinds of other ways and be generously ready to welcome them on your developmental path if and when they're ready.

Putting it all together

We all mature at different times and at different rates and rather than getting frustrated if your partner is ahead or behind you in theirs in any aspect, calm acceptance of the difference gives you both the freedom to continue at your own pace.

You're not in a competition. It doesn't matter if your partner isn't always up there with you on the personal development front. We reach stages in our maturing as and when we are ready. So being ready to wait unprotestingly, with no pressure on either side to progress faster or slower, lets you both off the hook and frees you to be yourselves.

The 'Take your tiger to the mountain' phrase is helpful in reminding you of this any time you're tempted to patronize your partner or to chivvy them to be more like you. It prompts you to enjoy your own progress and the place you are now wholeheartedly without worrying whether your partner understands your thinking and/or joins you there. It's ok to be different in the way and speed you mature. You are happy to wait for a time when and if they are ready to join you. Either way it's fine.

Patience accompanied by love and compassion for each other in your respective personal development feels calm and peaceful. It also encourages general understanding of each other's personality.

Take your tiger to the mountain whenever you feel any impulse to hurry up or slow down your partner's progress. All you have to think about is yours. Enjoy it and be content with the status quo of your relationship too.

37

Be upbeat and inspire one another

> 'The key is to keep company only with people who uplift you, whose presence calls forth your best.' Epictetus

> 'If you can dream it, then you can achieve it. You will get all you want in life if you help enough other people get what they want.' Zig Ziglar

> 'Go confidently in the direction of your dreams. Live the life you have imagined.' Henry David Thoreau

> 'You are never too old to set another goal or to dream a new dream.' C. S. Lewis

> 'As we let our own light shine, we unconsciously give other people permission to do the same. As we are liberated from our own fear, our presence automatically liberates others.' Marianne Williamson

Are you glass-half-full or glass-half-empty people? If the latter, I urge you with all my heart to change your demeanour and choose an upbeat one instead. It not only makes your life and your relationship a much nicer place to abide in, but it can transform them into a heaven on earth for your partner too.

'Heaven on earth? – isn't that pushing it?' you may be asking sceptically and my answer is absolutely, yes, you and your partner can create an atmosphere around you that feels heavenly, and no it isn't an exaggeration. Goodness and love and the potential to feel good is there for you every day. It's your opportunity and your choice to take it.

So often by default and/or others' example, or perhaps because we think it's somehow cool, we fall into a habit of being downcast. Just think for a minute, though, of the difference between an Eeyore (the rather dour donkey friend of Winnie-the-Pooh) type of person and someone upbeat. Just thinking of the doleful sort causes us to slump a little, or indeed a lot, if we don't watch out for it and decide not to. Meeting and spending time with someone cheerful, on the other hand, lifts our spirits effortlessly. You may think we can't choose to be like these happy souls. We can. You can. You may think you don't deserve to be happy. You do – we all do – we're given the gift of choice – it would be ungrateful to refuse it. Now reflect for a few moments on the usual demeanour of you and your partner when you're together and the affect your respective bearing has on each other. It isn't easy being with someone who tends to be downbeat, and if you're both like it happiness will seem like a vague dream you rarely experience. Yet every moment, every day, you can turn it around. Except in extreme circumstances of bereavement, difficulty and loss, you can meet every day with an upbeat attitude. It's your choice – you choose your attitude and you can choose to take an upbeat one. And just by being lighter, bright and cheerful, you will automatically affect the atmosphere around you both. Your partner can't help but be affected positively too. Inspire each other this way and happiness together is yours. It's an amazingly simple Secret for such an extraordinarily good result. Let's now look at some ways to do it.

DECIDE TO INSPIRE YOUR PARTNER

Decide that for today you will be an uplifting presence in any contact with your partner. Consciously flick the switch every time you lapse into worry, pessimism or any kind of needless negativity. Every time the temptation to be downbeat beckons – and it does for all of us sometimes – resist it and choose instead to take a positive, upbeat attitude. A negative approach is needless and unhelpful. There is always this option of positivity and it is your decision entirely to choose it. Don't irritate your partner by buzzing around them trying to make them happy though. Remember you can't make them or anyone else happy. It's their choice alone, just as your attitude is your choice.

But you can create an aura around you that will lighten the atmosphere in your whole environment simply by feeling and being upbeat. It's a choice every moment. Secret 29, Positivity pays dividends and Secret 36, Take your tiger to the mountain, will also be helpful in reminding you not to hassle your partner and to let them be.

Let your feeling of being upbeat and filled with inspiration do what it does best – make you a lovely person to be around – and it will feel wonderful for you too. For when you choose to be cheerful your aura will lighten the atmosphere around you and starts to uplift those around you, especially your partner who is so close to you, and naturally it lifts your own mood too. Notice and appreciate how good it feels when you're upbeat and decide to make it your default setting.

ENCOURAGE YOUR PARTNER TO BE UPBEAT TOO

Suggest to your partner that they be uplifting company for you too. Don't keep on about it – just remind them gently if ever they are being glum. This may make them laugh or scoff at you because until they try choosing a positive attitude they don't realize it's possible and feels so much better than negativity. So don't be offended if they laugh at you – laugh with them. That way you'll already be uplifting each other, so they will see immediately that it works. If they scoff, invite them to simply give a positive take on life a try. It's not that you're going to be always annoyingly trying to uplift each other with platitudes or over-the-top exuberance (fun though that is now and then!). It's simply making sure that they, like you, are upbeat and not doleful. Point out, too, that it isn't about being foolish. Positivity means you review options, realize there is always hope of a good outcome, and think constructively and energetically. Relentless negativity, on the other hand, embraces pessimism, even when there is scope to be constructive, and crushes possibility. Ask them to try it just for the day. To smile instead of scowl, to open their heart to possibilities of better instead of expecting the worst, to be encouraging and inspiring rather than being defeatist. The possibilities are endless of course. The key to feeling and being uplifting in all kinds of ways is to decide to be positive and then to experience how good it feels.

COUNT YOUR BLESSINGS OVER AND OVER AGAIN

Reflect on all the good things in life. We live in the most amazing world. Cherish the wonders of nature, of people, of all the wildlife. So much kindness and love if we bother to notice it. Be glad. See the splendours. In your home, your relationship, the wonder of being with the person you fell in love with. Love them now. Appreciate the small pleasures of life too. Let it all uplift you. Feel the updraft and your spirits rising with it and imagine you are in flow – enjoying life to the full. Suddenly you will realize you actually are. And all this happens whenever you decide to let it! Shine. Who are we not to? Whenever an attitude of gloom and doom threatens, be instantly alert to it and banish it decisively. Remember it helps to reflect on the myriad good things in life, appreciate all the love in your life and in your mind send out love to your partner and all you know. Keep counting your blessings and shine – just as they do.

Putting it all together

As the quote of Epictetus above reminds us, when we keep company with people who uplift us the world is a better place simply because their very upbeat presence makes it so. You can be that uplifting person around your partner, and they for you. There is absolutely no need for us to be constantly downbeat. Life is a mixture of events and influences and how we face them is up to us. How you are in your inner self and the self you show to the world, your demeanour reflected in your very being, is also your choice.

It feels much better to be upbeat. Not irrational, not unwisely optimistic, not false in any way but genuinely choosing to be up rather than down, constructive rather than destructive, hopeful and solution-seeking rather than defeatist by default. Upbeat feels good. It comes into being when we think it, choose it and let ourselves have the experience and joy of being it. As Marianne Williamson wrote, her words drawn on by Nelson Mandela in his inaugural speech, when we let our own light shine, we unconsciously give other people permission to do the same. We unbind ourselves from our fear that being upbeat is somehow wrong or dangerous and our presence then helps free others too. Shine, both of you. It doesn't just uplift each of you individually – you'll inevitably give each other the opportunity to look at the world in a different way – gladly and appreciatively. You'll give them permission to self-inspire as you inspire yourself. Do so every single day of your life and feel the happiness it gives you both – glow in your relationship.

38 Laugh together

> 'Never let the gentle stream of affectionate irony slip into the cold, dangerous waters of sarcasm.' Tim Lott

> 'There is nothing in the world so irresistibly contagious as laughter and good humour.' Charles Dickens

> 'Laughter is the sound of the soul dancing.' Jarod Kintz

> 'Laughter is more than just a pleasurable activity... When people laugh together, they tend to talk and touch more and to make eye contact more frequently.' Gretchen Rubin

> 'Let us always meet each other with [a] smile, for the smile is the beginning of love.' Mother Teresa

Laughter! Gosh it feels good. And it's amazingly healing. I've just had proof of this – in a stressful moment just now trying to sort out a tangle of detail, the other person and I found something to laugh about and it instantly put everything in perspective and made us both feel so much better. Just think how often in a relationship it can be good. Whenever you or your partner are tired, fraught about something, even in a dispute or in sadness, the ability to find something to smile about lightens the atmosphere and your mood giving precious respite, which even if it's just for a moment or two is always beneficial and can often dissolve tension and/or transform negativity to positivity.

It works in three ways: the physical part of laughing and smiling have a measurable effect on the brain as they trigger the release of feelgood hormones, including endorphins and oxytocin. Having a hug or even just enjoying a warm touch increases the response. It's also good for your heart rate, circulation and for relaxing generally, so that stress-induced or exacerbated illness stands to be relieved and perhaps even completely healed. Emotionally, of course, you're much more likely in any case to feel like being loving if you laugh together. And last but not least, having a laugh or even a wry comment that makes you smile, enables your brain to think more rationally – instead of feeling you're doomed, you realize that you can still laugh and lighten up and that's bound to make you feel better.

If you are saying that you can't possibly laugh when you're stressed or unhappy or generally going through a terrible time, please just try it out. I guarantee that laughing or smiling will in some way alleviate your stress. And please don't assume that you couldn't laugh even if you wanted to – you can. My mum nursed in the army in wartime and saw physical and emotional wounds no one should have to deal with. She and her colleagues largely coped, she often told me, with the help of the release of the laughter they shared with each other and their patients. It's a safety valve in our general lives, too, and especially in our relationships. Let's look at how you can not only enjoy laughter spontaneously, but make it your ally at will.

RE-CREATE THE WAY YOU USED TO LAUGH TOGETHER

Once again, I'd like to take you back to the early days of your relationship. You laughed a lot. You smiled at each other too. Above all, you loved to make each other smile and laugh. Then the seriousness of life and familiarity intervened and you may have found you don't do that as much as you used to. Bring it back, big time, into your relationship today. And if you do still love to amuse each other, appreciate it to the full. Laughter given and shared is a treasure beyond valuation in your relationship. Enjoy it, of course, but also appreciate how good you continue to feel afterwards – endorphins and similar chemicals continue to circulate for a long while after whatever it was that produced them. Appreciate, too, the way you tend to feel more loving and warm towards each other.

So make having fun and laughing together a major feature of your relationship now and for always. Don't wait for spontaneous humour – invite it in and practise it lots and lots, every day. Treasure the laughter you share with your partner and as you do it will bubble up inside you along with love. If you're interested in the science of it, as you enjoy it to the full, appreciate how good it is for your health. For as you laugh and in the aftermath of laughter, a whole host of the feelgood hormones it releases circulate, doing you the power of good in all ways, body, mind and soul. Appreciate the sense of wellbeing it brings to your relationship too. Feel the love and warmth.

SEEK OUT OPPORTUNITIES FOR HUMOUR

Look for the humour in all situations. Think of cartoonists – like many medics, they find humour even in the direst of circumstances. (Of course, if it's inappropriate to laugh at the time, store the funny thought for later when you're alone together and won't upset anyone who wouldn't get the joke.) I stress that I don't mean, ever, malicious humour. As Tim Lott pointed out above, there's a big difference between affectionate irony or any kind of humour and cold sarcasm or teasing designed to hurt. Sure it's fine to laugh at yourselves – but never, ever, nastily. Instead, find things to laugh about that please you both. As you start looking for humour, you'll come across it more and more and it's fun to think 'Oh I must remember that for John (or Jane)' and as you do you'll see them in your mind's eye breaking into a smile or a chuckle. This way you enjoy laughter with your partner three ways – beforehand, during and afterwards as you continue to relish the good feeling it gave and still gives you. Laughter draws you close and blows any blues away. Just remember never to use it as a weapon but always as a healer and peacemaker. Laugh with, not at each other and enjoy using laughter unabashedly to blow those blues away.

PRACTISE INDUCING LAUGHTER

Practise the art of laughing easily and often. There are all kinds of ways to induce laughter even if you're feeling flat or down. Imagining the feeling is one way. If you recall a time when you had a real chuckle or laughed until tears came to your eyes (in a good way) you will unconsciously bring the feeling back into your mind and body.

The feeling is seductive – you'll want to feel it more and more. Pretending to laugh is good too (please note again that I don't mean laughing falsely or nastily). It's been proven again and again that if we pretend to have a fit of the giggles, laughing aloud just as though we are, we pretty soon find the laughter is for real. Think, for example, of the laughing policeman song or the many examples of helpless giggling to be found on YouTube. Just go with it, laugh out loud and let it take you over, gloriously. It's brilliant even when self-induced like this.

The very act of laughing, however it comes about, causes the wonderful physiological responses (see above) that feel so, so good especially when shared. Similarly the very act of smiling, like laughter, automatically triggers the release of feelgood chemicals. Just try it. It works! When you laugh together it's especially good as the shared experience draws you close. Actually this happens even if one of you is laughing; the other will be pleased you're having such a fit of the giggles and feel the same rush of love for you as if they were immersed in them too. Laughter is better than any recreational drug at giving you a fix of happiness and a wonderful surge of love for each other. Let go, laugh – and love each other to bits.

Putting it all together

In any basically good relationship, laughter is the icing on the cake, and it's a great healer and restorer of love and concord too. When things are fraught or sad it gives respite, lightening your tension. It's one of heaven's blessings and it's not only free but your choice. Don't fall out of the habit of making each other laugh. For it is a habit you can look after and cherish. Never let a day go by without sharing some smiles and laughter. It feels great, lifts your spirits, draws you close. And when laughter becomes spontaneous and you let it take you over, the feeling of irresistibly chuckling or giggling is the most amazing tonic. It's infectious too, so if one of you gets the giggles, the other will too. Let yourselves go – it's totally brilliant.

As we saw above, we can coax laughter into our lives whenever we like, even if nothing outside of ourselves has made us laugh. Simply by pretending to laugh and going through the motions we open ourselves out to the real thing. All it needs is for you to invite that wonderful feeling into you and give yourself permission to let go and enjoy and it takes over.

It's a kind of generosity. When you laugh you're being generous to yourself – giving yourself the gift of a wonderful emotion and irresistible pleasure, and giving your partner the chance to laugh with you. Be generous to each other too – appreciate each other's witticisms and jokes, see the funny side, laugh and enjoy to the full! It's lovely when someone thinks we're funny – especially our nearest and dearest, and it makes us love them all the more.

Laughter is a bridge to healing, provides fresh perspective, restores your equilibrium. All make your relationship a more comfortable, happier place to be. Let it bubble up and enjoy the bliss.

(39) The fine art of compromise

> 'A good compromise, a good piece of legislation, is like a good sentence; or a good piece of music. Everybody can recognize it. They say, "Huh. It works. It makes sense."' Barack Obama

> 'Compromise and tolerance are magic words.' Hedy Lamarr

> 'I consult, I listen and I compromise where it's in the best interest.' Kamla Persad-Bissessar

> 'Provided that the balance is good, what you lose in compromise, you gain by collaboration.' Mike Rutherford

> 'The super power that I would choose would be compassion. Because that's what I think it takes to make it through life – an understanding, a give and take. It saves an awful lot of resentment.' Craig T. Nelson

A willingness to compromise is essential in almost every relationship as it's rare for two people to have evenly matched purpose and strength of will and they vary at different times of life too. If one person gets their own way consistently it smacks of inequality, perhaps dominance and even bullying. The ability to compromise is an essential part of fairness and loving thought for each other. It will be a fine balance you discover in your interaction, for like every couple you are individuals in a unique relationship. One happy couple I know have extremely different personalities in this regard. He is strong willed and makes a lot of noise and bluster about it. She is equally strong willed but quieter and patient. They both know they will reach agreement – in time and as apt for the particular situation, but they get around to reaching the compromise in their own style.

It's the same with give and take. Sometimes you may decide that actually it's fine to let your partner have their own way this time, or alternatively you might ask them to go with your choice if you're sure it's the better way.

It's not about being weak or strong. Being flexible is certainly a key to diplomacy but of course as all politicians are all too well aware, there are times when conceding a decision to the other party also concedes defeat. Diplomacy in a happy relationship, however, is never about being a winner or a loser. You reach an agreement you both agree to, and neither of you is coerced into doing something totally against your principles – it's a matter of finding the right way for the two of you in a particular set of circumstances.

The Secret of effective, fair compromise takes a lot of sensitivity and understanding of yourselves as well as each other.

Compromise takes compassion, a willingness to reconsider from all viewpoints and negotiation skills. You'll know when you've hit the right balance because it will feel right to both of you. Hold out for that right balance always. It will not only strengthen the bond between you but give you happiness too.

BE AWARE OF YOUR EGO BEING A PEST

Whenever we're thinking selfishly or irrationally we need to recognize that it's our ego making demands rather than common sense and logistics or a principle that's important to you. So, always, if you are protesting 'I'm right!' or 'I want!' or if you simply feel anxious about the wisdom of compromising, pause to think rationally and ask yourself:

- Is my ego preventing me, and
- Is my wounded or spoilt inner child demanding attention?

Now taking these potential blockers out of the equation if they are present, ask yourself: 'Would compromising actually be the best way forward?'

Look at the question totally objectively and be as rational, compassionate, honest and fair as possible. Finally, if you are still troubled, ask yourself: 'Does it sit well with my integrity and authenticity?' If compromising on the issue would also mean compromising your inner truth, then you need to stand firm. Otherwise, if common sense tells you flexibility is the best way forward, go for it! When you take your ego and spuriously hurt feelings, you can easily see if compromise is a good solution. Always be rational and scrupulously fair. If compromise is clearly – as it usually is – the obvious and best way forward, oust any temptation to play the martyr or to patronize each other and compromise willingly and positively.

THINK SOLUTION!

When compromising, keep solution focused. Remember that flexibility needs to be mutual in a relationship and can be in many forms, degrees and ratios depending on the situation. It doesn't have to be a radical 'give' or 'take' – often a slight adjustment of terms can ease the embargo and give a promise of a solution agreeable for you both.

Think how it would be if you shifted your stance a little to accommodate your partner's interests. A little bit more needed, perhaps? Or should you meet in the middle? Again, you might this time consider letting them have their own way in this, or the lion's share with some of your thinking incorporated. You might find yourself saying, once you've thought about it logically and unemotionally: 'It would be fine for them to make the decision and choice this time.' It all depends. So consider all angles with an open mind while remembering to be solution focused. An easy way to do this is to seek an answer to the question: 'What is the best way for this to work out and go ahead for both of us?' Flexibility, an open mind, and lots of give and take make finding a mutually good solution even easier. And working together to find it draws you close.

STAND UP FOR YOURSELF AND FOR FAIRNESS

Worth a check, every now and then, to ensure you're not always the one making the decisions while your partner compromises, or vice versa. Remember, a relationship that's truly happy for each of you is a democracy with an equal sharing of giving and taking. It's fine to settle for an easy life sometimes but not always. I know couples where one or other monopolizes the TV control device, for instance, or where one partner always eats the other's choice of food, subjugating their own preferences. Small controls indeed, but they pave the way for general dominance. It isn't fair, and even if the controlled one accepts it, underneath they will be inevitably harbouring a deep-seated sense of the unfairness of it and this could turn to resentment at any time. So stand up for yourself and make sure your partner isn't continually coerced by you either. There's always a way around things even if you don't agree. For instance take turns in what you like or with a little planning accommodate both. Remember – be generous, compassionate and fair. You are equals who love each other – incorporate these two characteristics of your relationship in all decisions and every compromise. Bear in mind though that continually giving way isn't healthy for relationship happiness and when you really don't want to agree on a compromise as such, find a way of dealing with your respective points of view that you can each accept. It's a bit like being on a seesaw – work together to keep the movement comfortable and protect your equality by constantly adjusting the balance of give and take.

Putting it all together

Compromise is a solution for both of you. When you cherish each other, you guard your equality and together look for a good balance in decision-making, adjusting willingly as befits the situation. Be conscious that one or other of you (and this might reverse at different stages of your life together) probably has a tendency to take control and guard against allowing yourself or your partner always getting their own way while the other compromises

Flexibility normally is best when it's mutual and willing with lots of kindness, care and even-handedness in the mix. You'll know you've hit on the right balance of give and take when it feels right to both of you and you can even, at least most of the time, be enthusiastic about the way forward. Be ready to be the instigator of negotiations. Your example will encourage your partner to join you in seeking solutions. Be content to be the initial peacemaker too, and to follow your partner's lead when they are the first to start negotiating. As you work together, diplomacy has the brilliant effect of drawing you together as a couple. It reminds you that you are a team by mutual choice and that it feels good to seek resolution and a positive way forward. When you compromise, do it generously and don't look back. Embrace the path you've chosen and move forward together gladly. Feel the happiness around and between you both.

40 Think love, choose love

> 'Love is always bestowed as a gift – freely, willingly and without expectation. We don't love to be loved; we love to love.'
> Leo Buscaglia

> 'Lord, grant that I might not so much seek to be loved as to love.' St Francis of Assisi

> 'Love seeks one thing only: the good of the one loved. It leaves all the other secondary effects to take care of themselves. Love, therefore, is its own reward.' Thomas Merton

> 'Do all things with love.' Og Mandino

> 'Love doesn't just sit there, like a stone; it has to be made, like bread, remade all the time, made new.' Ursula K. Le Guin

Beckon love into your relationship and encourage it to stay. Can you really invite love into your life, your very being? Absolutely. Certainly, love sometimes arrives out of the blue – spontaneously and unconditionally – for instance when a parent sees/hears/holds their newborn baby and at the beginning of a relationship. But it's rare, other than at peak emotional times like this, that love stays steadfastly strong without our conscious input. For love usually starts with a thought and continues with the wish that it should and the will to do our very best to help it do so.

So whether love initially comes to us as a spontaneous feeling or a consciously registered thought and decision, we need each

174

day to nurture and appreciate it to fulfil its promise and amazing, life-enhancing potential. We choose, most times, to love. And like us, love flourishes when it's chosen – and loved. Can you love love? Definitely! Like any emotion we can be aware of it and enjoy it – we can love it with our whole hearts and, knowing we do, make sure we do everything we can to keep it at the forefront of our minds in everything we do. It enhances every aspect of life if we remember to act lovingly but in a relationship it's of course especially important, for the first premise of your relationship is that you love each other. Why else be together? Money, status, parenting are reasons for staying together, certainly, but fundamentally you know in your heart that what you and your partner want, underpinning your whole life together and running through it as a feelgood current, is to love each other, passionately, steadfastly, romantically and practically.

Ah – practically. This is the key to all the types of love in your relationship. Love isn't airy-fairy, a dream, wishful thinking. It's a real, everyday decision you and your partner both need to make to feel love every day for each other and to act lovingly. We think it into being. We choose to love, decide to and then follow it through. It's easiest to love when the love between you is still thriving but it's possible to invite it back if it's gone missing. Neglect of love lets it go, attention and loving care brings it into being. It's up to you and your partner. And it's the greatest gift you can give each other and receive.

ACTIVATE YOUR LOVE

In counselling, I find that partners who aren't getting on or who are even apparently at daggers drawn with each other usually answer, if asked: 'Yes I do love him (or her).' Then, inwardly, I breathe a sigh of relief, for where there's love, there's hope. And where there's love there should and can be great happiness. But in our busy lives it's easy to let the day's events take over and neglect love or forget it altogether. Don't let this ever, or ever again, happen to you and your partner.

Instead, keep love at the forefront of your minds. It is, after all, the most important thing in your life and is as essential for your relationship as your individual selves. Bring the feeling of love consciously to mind right now and make it your firm intention for the day ahead. Pause to feel it. If it's absent and you can't, then imagine it. You know the feeling well – just recall it and sink into imagining it and relishing how it feels. It's a great feeling to love – let yourself go. Remember it. Feel it now. Recall that your partner is the person you choose to share your life with, your most intimate moments, yourself. Let the feelings of love transfuse your thoughts. Just love them, pure and simple, however they happen to be at the moment and even if they are being really difficult. Smile, think positively and let love deal with it. You'll become aware of a good way of responding. Love is like that – it affects a situation and often transforms it in a good way, always.

So just remember, often and whenever it goes AWOL (absent without leave) to think love. In so doing you recall its existence and activate it. If it's dormant, it will awaken. If it's lying low, you will up the ante and re-energize it. If it's in a great place right now, keep it there by appreciating it to the full. Let love transfuse your thoughts and your being. Bring it actively into your responses to each other and any situation you're in together. Over and over again, think love. Make it your raison d'être – your way of being, your reason for being. Love feels good and it's at the heart of relationship happiness.

MAKE LOVE YOUR CHOICE

Remember that loving, like all the Secrets, is your choice and that it's the one that makes all the others more viable and more pleasurable. Whatever you do, wherever you are, you choose how you are going to react to your partner and the situations in which you find yourselves. When you let negative feelings dictate your responses, they add to the negativity. Think love instead. With love in your mind, the way you interact with your partner and respond to the current issues will affect them just as directly in a positive way.

As in the last Secret, beware your ego butting in. Ego can be inclined to rather like the drama of the fight and tell you you're being spirited and clever. Ego likes the excitement of being horrid to each other and enjoys telling you that you are in the right. Dismiss it summarily and replace it with love. Quieter and more subtle it undoubtedly is than heated, ego-driven exchanges of anger, but the positive effect of it is huge and will heal and enhance your interaction and your relationship as a whole. Choose it every step of the way, every day. Whenever negativity is ruling you, think love instead. Whenever your ego is ruling you, think love instead. Remember the positive effect a loving and positive attitude has and let it lead and heal your interaction with your partner.

IF LOVE SEEMS IRRETRIEVABLE, FIND OUT WHY

If active loving behaviour towards each other seems difficult in your relationship's current state or at any time, step back from the immediate hassle and take an overview of the whole picture. See what's going wrong and how. Is the negative interaction really about the two of you or caused by external influences? So often, we let our own emotional or practical anxieties affect our prime relationship when it actually has nothing to do with it. Once you (and/or your partner) have identified where the negative feeling affecting your ability to proactively love each other is coming from, have some quiet time alone together and tell each other about it and how you're feeling. Shared, the difficulty will not only be easier to circumnavigate whenever it's threatening your closeness and love but will have the effect of drawing you together instead. If there's a problem between you, again, talk it over and see how you can resolve it positively and constructively. (See Secrets 3, 4 and 10.) Communicating your thoughts and feelings to each other enables understanding and mutual compassion and empathy. Again this will draw you closer, heal hurt and enable you to reactivate your proactive lovingness for each other. Above all, whatever your differences, bring love back into the picture and as it illuminates it feel the renewed warmth between you. Love each other. 100 per cent.

Putting it all together

To love truly is all we need and it is all around us. When we bring love into our very being and all our behaviours, it transforms everything we do and our interaction with everyone we meet. This is never more so than with our partners.

Feel love. Give love. Seek only good for your partner, always. Do this and you will surround yourself with an atmosphere of inner contentment and defuse or dissolve any negative feelings swirling around inside you. Being human, of course, despite your best efforts at this, there'll probably be times when loving feelings, let alone behaviour, still seem to be temporarily unattainable.

Then get out for a brisk walk, punch some pillows, or do something you love doing – whatever it takes to calm yourself and get back your sense of perspective and kindness.

Love is always there, waiting for you to let it flood through you again.

Let it. Feel it. Love it.

Love each other with your whole heart – it is one of life's richest blessings and greatest joys.

41 Trust

'The best way to find out if you can trust somebody is to trust them.' Ernest Hemingway

'Have enough courage to trust love one more time and always one more time.' Maya Angelou

'As we fly, we still may not know where we are going to. But the miracle is in the unfolding of the wings. You may not know where you're going, but you know that so long as you spread your wings, the winds will carry you.' C. JoyBell C.

'None of us knows what might happen even the next minute, yet still we go forward. Because we trust. Because we have Faith.' Paulo Coelho

'We are all mistaken sometimes; sometimes we do wrong things, things that have bad consequences. But it does not mean we are evil, or that we cannot be trusted ever afterward.' Alison Croggon

When you trust your partner, and they you, you give each other the gift of respect for their integrity, belief in their strength to withstand temptation and, above all, you give them your love. This mutual vote of confidence bonds you deeply. It boosts your self-esteem as well as the regard you have for your partner.

When you trust someone, you take a leap of faith. There is no guarantee it will be upheld, but that doesn't stop us trusting all will be well and our trust is, in the main, well placed. We trust people with our lives every day – for instance, our fellow road users and the manufacturers of the appliances we use. We know they could make or have already made mistakes that could cost us dear and perhaps even kill us, yet we take the view that there's a very strong chance that all will be well and so we implicitly put our faith in them. How much more so can you and your partner put your faith in each other when you know you are each other's dearest loved one? They love, respect and care deeply for you, and you them, and you have pledged that you will both do your level best to carry through and be worthy of each other's trust. And yet it's very easy to have doubts and then suspicions become more invasive and threaten our trust. Which you go with is your choice and given that doubt and suspicion feel dangerous and dire, and trust feels safe and lovely, trust is the outright winner. Not only that, but if you trust your partner, they are far more likely to summon the will and courage to be dependable and trustworthy.

What if your partner has betrayed your trust – is it possible for you to trust them again, knowing full well they could do so again, however vehemently they promise not to?

Yes, it's perfectly possible. Unless your partner has let you down over and over again, you make the same leap of faith in trusting them as the first time. We are all fallible. We all deserve to be forgiven. (For more on this, see Secret 25, Forgive.) We are all capable of learning from our weaknesses or deliberate bad behaviour and promising to be strong and well behaved in future. Trust given and received gives each of you strength and, above all, it feels good.

BLESS EACH OTHER WITH THE GIFT OF TRUST

Give yourself, your partner and your relationship the benediction of trust. It is a gift to yourself, too, for the conscious decision to trust your partner frees you from the negative effects of suspicion and distrust. Don't put conditions on it. Just trust in the power of loyalty and goodness. Feel the anxiety and fear dropping away from you and register how good it feels to be able to relax. Be very aware of the sense of freedom it gives you from the exhausting tyranny of doubts and misgivings.

If they threaten again for no reason other than your own fear, think of the powerful, benevolent nature of trust and send the doubt and associated anger packing. Be aware of the effect it has on your partner too when they are freed from the anxiety inevitably caused by you doubting their willpower and living in a state of fear. Once you've opted to trust, stop thinking about it and let it be the default setting that flows quietly and steadfastly through your relationship. Trust each other unreservedly and feel how good it is to be able to relax. Remember not to clutter your trust with conditions or to keep checking up to see if it's upheld. By trusting generously and wholeheartedly you'll prevent suspicion and doubt taking hold again. Don't entertain them for an instant. Trust each other. In the freedom of trust, you are both far more likely to be trustable and to live together loyally and honestly.

WHEN TRUST IS NEVERTHELESS BETRAYED, DEAL WITH IT SENSIBLY AND CONSTRUCTIVELY

When your trust has been repeatedly betrayed, despite pledges not to let you down again, it's important to look after yourself. I recommend getting help for your partner and yourself. You could consider having relationship counselling, or, if an addiction or compulsive behaviour is involved, they may be helped by specialist counselling or group therapy. Be aware of all the implications and be scrupulously logical about them. Be sensible in not getting sucked in again when there seems little reason to trust again. But remember that people can learn and change even though they've gone wrong many times. An alcoholic, for instance, or a serial adulterer, may relapse but then go on to succeed in giving up their addiction. I stress again that they usually need back-up help to do this though. Renounce blame and shame and instead encourage and believe in their ability to be trustable. And – as in Secret 40 – think love. Together with trust, it can heal and renew. As well as insisting your partner seeks help, consider relationship counselling. Also, as to whether you stay together or separate, the experience will impact your equilibrium and wellbeing so seek counselling or group therapy for yourself in coping with your partner's behaviour.

Remember that there is always hope for learning change and renewed strength and that trust in the possibility of healing is more conducive to it and the restoration of your happiness, whether on your own or together, than blame and shame.

TRUST NOW. DON'T KEEP REPLAYING PAST HURTS AND GRIEVANCES

Remember that the present is now and the future starts here too. (See Secret 5.) Don't waste time and emotion on replaying past hurts and fears – you'll only invite them to stay in your relationship and sabotage your happiness now. Treat every day as a new beginning. If your partner has hurt you, blame and shame won't help. Focus instead on the love between you and your ongoing choice to be and stay together. Think, together, how you can constructively help yourselves be strong and withstand temptations that would negatively affect each other. Think of trust as a liberator that frees you both to behave well because you want to and can, not because you feel forced to. Replace suspicion and fear of misplaced trust with confidence in your partner and belief in the possibility that your trust is well placed.

Focus on your love and desire to be together and constructively think, together, how you can help yourselves behave lovingly and well towards each other. See trust as your friend and ally. Since it assuredly is.

Putting it all together

Trust is the seed of hope and faith, the nourishing oxygen of willpower, the seal of approval that will cheer you both on to keep behaving lovingly and caringly. When we trust we banish suspicion and doubt that – untreated – grow, preventing you from enjoying your relationship to the full and threatening your love for each other.

Trust is a hug of recognition – that your partner is an autonomous being and you believe they choose to be loving and caring towards you. It's all tied up with mutual respect and the freedom you both have. Always remember, when doubt pops up, that your partner loves you just as you love them – that's why you decided to be together and, every day, reaffirm that decision.

A lack of trust betrays the essence and foundations of your relationship. Whether or not you've a formal commitment such as marriage, when you decided to be an item you tacitly or actually agreed to love, honour and cherish each other. Trust is implicit in those promises – without it they are empty, with it they can shine bright for ever through hard times and even occasional lapses from the good behaviour you've pledged.

We all need encouragement and the faith of our partner is the most comforting and inspiring gift we can receive. Accept it with pride and give it generously with joy in your heart.

It frees you both to be good to each other of your own accord – because you want to be and know you can be.

Finally, but very importantly, the feelgood nature of trust enables you to love wholeheartedly and to accept your partner's love. Giving and receiving love (Secret 40) is the lifeblood of a relationship and the reason you are together. Trust each other, and let love – and happiness – flow.

42 Rid yourself of petty annoyances

❝ 'After you criticize someone, you'll notice that you will feel a little deflated and ashamed, almost like you're the one who has been attacked. The reason this is true is that when we criticize, it's a statement to the world and to ourselves: "I have a need to be critical."' Richard Carlson

❝ 'He was always afraid she'd let loose with her ridiculous laugh, which was like fingernails on a blackboard for him. Though the couple had a great deal in common, their connection slowly eroded because of this quirk. After 15 years of marriage, however, the wife developed cancer and died. Now he yearns to hear that laugh just one more time.' Dr John Buri

❝ 'Changing your perspective can not only resolve the irritating issue, it can mend the dynamic of the whole relationship.' Rosie Hallett

❝ 'Do unto others as you would be done to.' The New Testament

❝ 'Nothing like holding up a mirror and looking into it to see how annoying we're being.' Anon

As you are two people with your own unique personalities, it's inevitable that you will annoy each other sometimes, especially as you are in a relationship where you spend so much time together. Realizing that it's normal to be irritated sometimes is the key to dealing with it positively, so that it doesn't spoil your interaction and eat away at your love. It's tempting to pretend we're not aggravated or aggravating as we long for a perfect relationship. But once we realize that no one is perfect and it's normal to exasperate each other sometimes, we can see it's no big deal because we can defuse it safely before it becomes bothersome.

One of the secrets of avoiding being irritating is, of course, to admit that you can be. When you see your quirks and habits through your partner's eyes it can be quite a shock! So every now and then take a look at yourself as though through their eyes.

Friends may smile indulgently or ignore our troublesome traits, but they're not with us for long tracts of time and every day. Not so easy to turn a blind eye when you're living with someone. So it's a good idea to regularly – and whenever you sense you're irritating your partner – to take a raincheck on your behaviour.

A great question to ask yourself is: 'Am I being or behaving in a way I wouldn't have dreamed of when we were going out?' And if you realize you've let yourself go, whether that's in appearance, attitude or behaviour, you owe it to yourself and your partner to put it right.

And when you're irritated by your partner, remember the rose-coloured glasses you unconsciously wore when you first got together. Their foibles seemed endearing then and, madly in love, it never occurred to you that one day they'd get on your nerves. But, hey, it's just one of those things that happens as the allure of first attraction turns into everyday love. Again, facing up to it is hugely helpful. Then you can consciously put your rose-coloured glasses back on so your attitude shifts into a fondly tolerant one. This is the person you love truly and deeply – does it really matter if they have a few tics and traits? Couldn't you just shrug off the annoyance you feel and be more easy-going about it? Being critical and impatient doesn't feel pleasant. Kindness and acceptance feel great. So when you let go of feeling aggravated, you both benefit hugely.

NOTICE YOUR OWN QUIRKS AND HABITS

Take a look at yourself often through the eyes of others – and especially through those of your partner. See your foibles and habits clearly. Now remember how you controlled or hid them when you were first together. The big question to ask yourself is: 'Would I have done this thing in front of them then?' It's useful, whenever you sense you are irritating your partner, to hold a mirror up to your behaviour and look at it. Yes, that's you. Do you really want/need to continue the behaviour? Monitoring our behaviour to make sure we're not being offensive or coming across as unthoughtful and uncaring of their feelings is a common courtesy and a mark of respect for their feelings. You curb your less attractive habits when with friends, so just think how even more important it is to do so with your partner. This of course works both ways. If your partner has a habit that you'd really like them to lose, get them to see it through your eyes. Thinking how you each look to others is a great monitor of unpleasant or needlessly annoying quirks. Without being too self-conscious or self-obsessed, keep a watchful eye on the picture you present to others and, especially, your partner.

Be pleasant, polite and thoughtful with each other – it shows you value each other's opinion and saves a lot of needless annoyance.

EASY WAYS TO GIVE UP OR CURB IRRITATING BEHAVIOUR

Break an irritating pattern with playfulness. Good-hearted shared laughter is a great way to take the wind from the sails of a stubbornly continued annoying habit. It can highlight how others see it, instead of making the partner with the habit hurt and defensive and seeing you as mean or intolerant. It needs to be good-hearted of course to avoid them feeling mocked or belittled, so throw lots of love into the mix. Then you can look at it objectively.

Another way, if you know your partner is grumpy about something you do even though you think it's trivial, is to empathize with the background to their moodiness. Could they, for instance, assume you don't have much regard for them because you keep repeating the behaviour they dislike? If so, reassure them you do love them and admit it's engrained behaviour. Or is their irritation a hark-back to someone else's lack of love or care? Once this is out in the open you'll find it easier to give it up or control it when with them, and/or they will be much more likely to get any unfair irritation into perspective. Ask yourselves 'Is this really terribly important in the present between the two of us?'. If it isn't, let the irritation go. If it is, banish the habit.

ACCEPT YOU'RE SURE TO HAVE SOME BEHAVIOURAL DIFFERENCES

Remember to be aware that you are two individuals. You had different upbringings in your own families. You've matured in different ways since. You're bound to behave differently and have some dissimilarities in your customs and quirks. Give each other plenty of leeway to be yourselves and don't try to foist your ways on to your partner. Find some middle ground where you can, and where you can't, accept differences and in the latter case discuss them kindly and constructively. With smaller, essentially unimportant aggravations, smile at them instead of letting them annoy you or shrug them off completely, remembering they're not immensely important in the great scheme of things. Be prepared to give and take with lots of leeway on the 'right' way to behave. Or simply say Vive la différence!

Remember that you were once totally enchanted with each other. Essentially you are still the same two people. So get back that attitude of love and admiration. A bonus is that when we feel appreciated we're encouraged to behave well, so we 'earn' each other's love all the more. Mutual admiration and approval, generously given, encourages you both to behave well and lovingly. And that, as well as helping you both give up any unwanted foibles, feels really good.

Putting it all together

Love can flourish when you both take care not to offend each other's sensibilities. It's not about suppressing your personality or being controlled — it's about caring for yourself as well as your partner. To others, we are the person they see and hear. If we paint a picture of someone carelessly or, worse, deliberately being annoying, we're bound to be irritating and are actually letting ourselves down. We owe it to ourselves, life and love to be and make the very best of ourselves. We do it automatically when we're first in love but the intimacy of living together can lead us to forget. Remember always that while love adapts and adjusts, we want the person we're with to still essentially be the lovely, fragrant in all ways person we first fell for. Mutual tolerance of the way our behaviour changes as we grow and mature is great. But it needs to go hand in hand with respect for each other's feelings and a deep-seated wish to love and to be lovable. That means behaving well and caring for each other's perception of us – see Secrets 15, 17 and 32.

We all have different family customs and levels of thought on what constitutes acceptable behaviour and appearances. So yes, apply lots of give and take. It works both ways so takes input from you both to avoid being irritating as much as possible, and to exercise acceptance and give generous leeway as much as you can when you feel irritated. We are all irritating to our partners sometimes and we can all feel irritated by them! Compassion and courtesy work together to dissolve bad habits and promote tolerance and fond love and acceptance. With bucketloads of both see how your relationship shines and glows with mutual love and approval.

43 Get the keys to a great attitude to sex

CC 'We waste time looking for the perfect lover, instead of creating the perfect love.' Tom Robbins

CC 'Anyone who is in love is making love the whole time, even when they're not.' Paulo Coelho

CC 'Sex is an emotion in motion.' Mae West

CC 'To be open to love, to trust and believe in love, to be hopeful in love and live in love, you need the greatest strength.' Leo Buscaglia

CC 'Amazing sex stays with you. It soaks into your skin. It floats through your dreams and has you silently smouldering with delicious remembrances for hours after.' Roberto Hogue

Enjoyable and enjoyed, lovemaking adds a special dimension of pleasure and happiness into the mix of a relationship.

In the beginning it's spontaneous but once the in-love excitement settles, great sex is very much a proactive choice – or not of course. There are two possibilities for the future of your sex life. In one, you could spend less time making love and have intercourse less often and perhaps infrequently. But, with one of you probably less keen than the other, negative inborn attitudes may surface and then excuses tend to start and patterns change. Days, or even weeks or months may go by without sex and so it becomes a special occasion happening. If it is good, the one who's keener hopes it will bode well for more frequent lovemaking. If it isn't, interest probably wanes on both sides. Either you pretty much give up on sex, or one of you participates under duress. Either way, there'll be disappointment. It doesn't add to your relationship happiness.

The alternative way is fantastic: you can instead (at any stage of your relationship) realize that you can choose to put it at the forefront of your mind and, when you do, notice with delight that you begin – spontaneously – to feel sexy.

Beware at this point for, again, core negative attitudes may surface. If your mum or other role models have made faces or said things showing their opinion that sex is dirty or a chore, these memories, even subconsciously, can be all it takes for you to suppress your sensuality and decide you're too tired, don't feel like it after all, have a headache or pick on any one of a host of other reasons you won't have sex now.

Simply refuse to let this negative thinking stop your libido in its tracks. Use your mind to remind yourself that, actually, sex with the person you love is wonderful and once you get going you have a great time. It brings you closer, transfuses you with love for each other and releases a load of feelgood hormones that stay with you long into the next day.

It's all about your minds and your mutual decision to go for it.

Lovemaking is a skill that can give you exquisite pleasure but like any such skill, it's up to you to practise it. The rewards are huge in relationship happiness.

LET GO OF NEGATIVE PREJUDICE

Break free from old belief systems and negative patterns. Take an enquiring look at the attitude to sex you grew up with or have acquired since. First consider your long-held beliefs about sex and assess any negativity you may have. Then work out where they came from. Your parents whether consciously or unwittingly advocated their beliefs about sex. If they were negative in any way, you'd unconsciously have picked up on this and been imprinted with the negative vibe yourself. If, on the other hand, they were great enthusiasts, you may have been embarrassed or perhaps feel you don't measure up on the sensuality front. Or perhaps they simply didn't give you any clues to their thoughts on sex – lots of people even today prefer to keep completely private about it. In that case, where did you learn about sex? Doing a little detective work on where you got your impressions and ideas about sex is illuminating. From there you can use your own mind to relearn the attitude you want – that good sex with the partner you love is wonderful, healthy and very desirable emotionally and physically and adds a welcome dimension to the happiness of your relationship. You don't have to stay imprinted with a bad or sad attitude to sex. Choose a new way of thinking – that good sex is lovely, good for you, and brilliant for the happiness of your relationship too.

GIVE YOURSELF A POSITIVE, WELCOMING ATTITUDE TO LOVEMAKING

Imagine intensely, warmly pleasurable lovemaking. Go back in your mind and body to a session of sex you enjoyed. Be there imagining you and your partner as a couple deeply in love and mad about each other. Really feel all the sensations as you recall them. Love, for instance, the scent of your partner, the feel of them, their touch on you, the way you loved their body too, and feel vividly the waves of pleasure starting. Don't just dream of it in the past or hope for it again in the future – be there now in your mind. Feel the love, so strong between you. It is your reality now. You are still that same sensual, desire-carried person who adores making love and giving and receiving pleasure. Feel it. Love it. Love your partner and let them be the one you desire as intensely and passionately as you experienced desire then. Feel it and you are there; it's not just a memory or a dream – it's you now – your reality of being and feeling truly, adorably sexy and sensual. Let the thought and feeling of waves of pleasure wash over you and realize this is still you now and you can awaken yourself this way when you wish to. Your body will respond in kind for real, releasing the feelgood hormones of lovemaking even before you start to encourage yourself to go ahead and enjoy. Live in this reality and love it – just like you used to. And hey – perhaps even more?

REALIZE AND RELEASE YOUR SEXUAL POWER

You have the sensual and emotional talent to love sex, and the ability to release it. Feel your strength of will and the sensual power and ability of your body. Be aware that you have the physical and emotional and sensual capability and skill to decide to enjoy the full potential of the sexual side of your relationship. So open yourself, your mind and your body to the possibility of actively enjoying great lovemaking. Then it's just one step to deciding you're going to – not just willingly but proactively and enthusiastically. Put your all into it – that's to say not to over-do it with assumed passion (and perhaps scare your partner!) – but to show them you are warm and loving and receptive to their lovemaking. Let them know that you want to give them pleasure and enjoy the pleasure you have too. Decide to make love in good heart, lovingly, and with all your sensual input. Instead of shutting doors, open them. See and feel the possibility of enjoying your sensuality to the full and then take the next step and go ahead.

Enjoy making love your way – passively, proactively, however you feel you would like to. The key is enthusiasm and a willingness to enjoy yourself and help your partner enjoy the act too. Feel your warm, loving receptivity to the idea and the reality of making love – body, mind and soul. Giving and receiving pleasure gives you an amazing feeling of closeness and is one of the nicest aspects of happiness together. Above all, love as you are making love. Be the love you share – for good sex between loving partners is love in action

Putting it all together

Sexuality is elemental – a fundamental part of our being. Sadly, sex is mutated by a few into something else – a control device, pornography, something somehow shameful. You have the opportunity and ability at any stage of your life to claim or reclaim it as the wonderful source of intense, exquisite pleasure and expression of love it truly is.

It's up to the two of you. Together you can choose to enjoy it for its own earthy sake and also as a way of giving and sharing your love of each other.

Deciding to be up for it, willingly, enthusiastically and putting your heart into it as well as your body, takes in many aspects of the other Secrets. It's about, for instance, your belief in yourself and your wish to love each other to the full.

It's also about seeing it as the glorious gift it is. Another little bit of heaven in the heaven-sent miracle of loving your partner and choosing to share your life with them. Good sex comes in so many ways – with the mix probably changing somewhat as you move through life. It doesn't have to involve intercourse, for instance. It can be a loving touch, the readiness to, for example, gave your partner a massage, or to be happy to hold hands or put your arms round each other in public perhaps. It's about an openness and warmth that invite the other in and surround you both in an aura of sensuality and deep-seated love in all its elements.

Perhaps most of all it's the letting go of inhibitions and the busyness of life that can cause tiredness and the wish to 'do your own thing'. Not that there's anything wrong with having time and space of your own – we need that too – but your relationship is very, very precious and deserves some dedicated time and your full, open-hearted input.

Shared pleasure is the supreme way of sharing yourselves with each other. If you've lost touch with that pleasure or don't often make time for it, please get back in touch and take time. It will bring a special kind of happiness to you both – not just the pleasure, lovely though that obviously is, but in the way it draws you close, creates a special, unique bond between you, and gives a swing and lightness to your walk through this life – together.

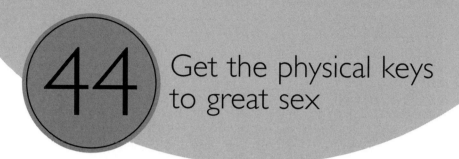

44 Get the physical keys to great sex

> 'Be prepared for your preferences to change throughout your lives.' Peggy & James Vaughan

> 'If you have had intimate sex during which you have been aware not only of yourself but also sensitive to your lover then you will feel lovingly close to him or her.' Anon

> 'Sex is always about emotions. Good sex is about free emotions; bad sex is about blocked emotions.' Deepak Chopra

> 'The way you make love is the way God will be with you.' Rumi

> 'Sex and intimacy can boost your self-esteem and happiness, too. It's not only a prescription for a healthy life, but a happy one.' Sheenie Ambardar

In Secret 43 we looked at how the overall key to enjoying a deeply pleasurable sex life is to open your mind to it, abandoning any psychological blocks and negative prejudices you were brought up with or have gathered along the way of life. This Secret goes on apace from there: it's about taking the opportunity you have to directly take the next step and discover the secrets of putting into practice your self-given freedom and inspiration to enjoy sex – and discovering how to have a great time together.

It's sometimes suggested that to have to learn the mechanics of sex takes away from the magic, but in fact it's the opposite: learn the secrets of great sexual techniques and like any learned skill and art after a while they become second nature. Then you can flow with them on waves of pleasure that uplift and carry you as naturally as can be. You may know them all already, in which case you can skip the whole of this Secret! Otherwise, go with the flow and enjoy. It's fun to read about the various suggestions, try them out and have a blissful time. They're worth revisiting now and then, as well. For over the years our bodies and minds change and we can find that the techniques that once we loved no longer transport us to sexual heaven. All the suggestions within this Secret are adaptable to any stage in life. You may even wish to give up on certain aspects completely one day. For various reasons, for instance, many people don't have intercourse but enjoy a deeply enjoyable and satisfying sex life nevertheless.

Take a look and consider how you can increase your spectrum of ability to give and receive pleasure. You have the gift of an incredibly complex body and nervous and neurological systems that work together in enabling the arousal curve from first thought through increasing pleasure to the greatest let-go feeling of all when you climax. It doesn't end there of course – the feelgood chemicals stay with you long afterwards. In modern parlance, what's not to like? Learn how and enjoy.

BECOME ORGASMIC

Learn how to have an orgasm easily, whenever you wish to. Become an expert at giving yourself orgasms. It's a skill you can learn and give yourself very easily. It's a gift to your partner too because once you know how to be orgasmic, you can show them the way. Even the best lover in the world can't 'give' you orgasms if you don't have the knack of letting yourself go, mind and body. Having a climax is a leap of faith, in a way, coupled with any one of countless triggers that work for some but not all, some of the time, but not always. Even for the most valiant and trusted of partners, it can be daunting to help someone learn this and if you were going to do it together you probably already have. But as you're reading this I'll assume you're not easily orgasmic yet and start at the beginning.

By far the easiest and most relaxed way to get to know your special way up the curve to climax and your triggers for that final bliss is to practise on your own. All you need is some solitude, around 30 to 60 minutes when you won't be interrupted, and your own touch and imagination. Enjoy trying out your touch to learn what pleases you, how your body responds and how, often with the added help of your imagination, you can increase arousal and tip over into climax at will.

This isn't the place for the details, but you can find full information about the orgasmic way with the help of my book *Orgasms and How to Have Them*. Getting good at it, so that it becomes easier and easier, is dependent on practise. It goes without saying that it's really enjoyable to do this and it will be your gift to yourself for the rest of your life and of course you and your partner within your relationship.

BRING THE GIFT TO YOUR LOVEMAKING

Once you're adept at having an orgasm when you wish, you can transfer the knowledge to your partner so that they know how to arouse you and take you through the curve to climax. If negative thoughts intrude and hinder your enjoyment, consciously let go of them and equally consciously decide to let your partner turn you on and take you over the orgasmic edge. Just as you can let yourself go into climax on your own, you can do so when you're making love. Think of it as giving them the key to turning you on and taking you through steadily growing arousal to the magical point where you go over the edge of pleasure into ecstasy. Good lovemaking is about giving pleasure as much as receiving it of course and you can do this simultaneously and/or in taking turns to focus on your own or your partner's enjoyment. With practise – and what can be better now you've decided and are ready to enjoy sex to the full – you may find you can climax at the same time. Though a lovely feeling, this isn't tremendously important – having a climax when the time is right for you is fine too. But as women tend to take longer than men to become fully aroused and climax, and as men usually like to rest after climaxing, it makes sense for the man to hold back until his partner has enjoyed hers and then let go into orgasm himself.

EMBRACE YOUR SENSUALITY

Use all your senses as you enjoy making love with your partner and be especially aware of them when they strike erotic chords. They are powerful aids in both letting go of inhibitions and in riding the arousal curve into orgasm. Vision, sound, touch, scent, imagination (the sixth sense) and above all your mind play roles, pleasurable in themselves, in the beauty, overall sensuality and sheer dynamism of great sex. Technically the path of desire starts in your mind with a thought about the possibility of making love. Be alert – notice it, welcome it and – as often as possible, say yes to it. But that initial thought can be triggered by a host of things that stir an erotic feeling – a beautiful painting or an unconsciously lovely movement or aspect of your partner, music you love, a scent that reminds you of great sex, a pleasurable touch – all can spark that thought of sex – the invitation to you to accept it and say yes to making love. Use your imagination too – fantasy is a hugely powerful aphrodisiac. Discover the ones that do it for you. And always remember your love for each other – it transcends the everyday pleasure of sex into an all-encompassing pleasure – body, mind and soul. Welcome the pleasure your senses give you and welcome your partner's lovemaking.

Invite your imagination in too – it's a wonderful aphrodisiac and often one of the keys to easy orgasms. Imagine that feeling of being highly aroused and you're almost there. Know which of the other aphrodisiacs at your disposal do it best for you too and, quite simply, thrill to the lovemaking you share – it's a glorious gift, body, mind and soul to yourselves, to each other and to your relationship.

Putting it all together

Sensual and sexual pleasure are closely linked and when you make love in the complete sense with your partner, they can take you to a heaven on earth. It's about letting go to pleasure and once you learn your own triggers and keys, you can do your partner and yourself the honour – and it is a very precious honour – of sharing your self-knowledge and of course learning theirs too. Freely, warmly, lovingly

197

and enthusiastically shared, the gift of good lovemaking gives you great happiness, and not just when you're making love but throughout your relationship generally. The feelgood hormones great sex generates permeate your general wellbeing and make you feel even better about the life, relationship and love you share.

Good sex not only draws you close, but causes your love to deepen and strengthen. It's a healer of emotional hurt, a boost to self-confidence and an all-round feelgood blessing. We can of course live without sex and be very happy. A relationship, too, can be very happy without sex. But loving, pleasurable sex is the icing on the cake and, in a relationship, an elixir for an increased sense of togetherness. It's a pleasure you can enjoy, in one form or another, all your life together. And all it takes is your decision to say yes to the gift – and enjoy it to the full.

45 Celebrate romance

❝ *'The word "romance" means excitement, adventure, and something extremely real. Romance should last a lifetime.'*
Billy Graham

❝ *'It's easy to get wrapped up in sharing everyday life with a partner. It's fun to get lost in love and romance. It's the best.'*
Brittany Murphy

❝ *'Love doesn't sit there like a stone, it has to be made, like bread; remade all of the time, made new.'* Ursula K. Le Guin

❝ *'While love is a beautiful expression of life, romance is a beautiful expression of love.'* Simran Khurana

❝ *'Love is the poetry of the senses.'* Honoré de Balzac

When romance lives throughout your years together it keeps the light of love sparkling, making the good times even brighter and illuminating the way in even the darkest ones.

Romance needn't be airy-fairy and dreamlike. The simplest of words and gestures express it, snapping it into life. 'I love you' is the heart of romance, of course, along with a loving touch or small gift. And it's so easy to be romantic in little things you say and do, every day.

A bit of romance or a lot is up to the preference of you and your partner. Overt abundance is loved by many; quiet unobtrusive romance by those who are more introvert. Most of us are probably somewhere in the middle, enjoying a gentle day-to-day love with a fairly low-key romantic backdrop and now and then expressing this in more extravagant displays.

It's precious in two ways: first it reminds you of the nature of your togetherness. Friends for sure, co-workers in earning your living, sexual partners, homemakers, parents perhaps – in all these romance is the spice that highlights and enhances the love that brought you together and keeps it shining bright. Second it feels lovely.

When you've let go of the romantic side of your love, you'll be aware that it feels as though love itself has faded slightly. Bring back the special light of passion and happiness it gives and keep it strong in your love and life together. In a sense, it's a way of giving thanks for these great gifts and shows you want them to last for ever. Romance signals you're still there loving each other, cherishing your days and nights together and relishing the special tenderness and joy you share.

It's sexy too. Every aspect of the sex Secrets is dusted with gold when romance is in the air. Quite simply, it makes it better.

So don't be cynical about romance ever. Treasure it for it is a great treasure in your relationship. It's all about happiness and it dances happiness into life. Use it liberally, your own way. Enjoy!

CHOOSE TO BE ROMANTIC

Think romantically. It's not hard, even for those who are habitually very down to earth. It's an easily acquired habit too, because it straightaway feels so good. Drive on through any initial awkwardness – the clunkiness won't spoil the overall feelgood factor – in fact it will highlight it rather well. To help, first clarify your understanding of romance. What does the word and the concept mean to you? Something associated with early love only – a touching thing that few keep later in life and which you yourselves have let go? Or even a totally novel concept for you as a couple perhaps? Actually it's a rather particular, heady, totally gorgeous aspect of love – the essence of love, pure and beautiful. It can feel hot and exciting; it can feel warm and cosy. It's very, very good and the great news is that it can be a constant part of the love and life you and your partner share.

People think of it as ephemeral but there's absolutely no need for it to be. And it's not fairy-story fantasy – you can indeed enjoy it as an integral part of your relationship for ever. It's entirely up to the two of you to nurture it.

So now consider this: why not make it a regular feature of your love life with your partner on an ongoing basis? I think you'll see easily there's no reason not to and, with the promise of added happiness, a huge incentive to go for it. So think now how you're going to do just that, starting today. Romance, like most aspects of love, starts in your minds. Remind yourselves the lovely meaning of romance and how good it is and keep it vibrant and flourishing in your togetherness.

Decide to make it a regular and ongoing feature of your life and your love. Don't ever be cynical about it – treasure it for it feels wonderful. Think romance. Be romantic!

MAKE TODAY AND EVERY DAY A TIME FOR ROMANCE

Make every day a romantic day. Choose from all kinds of romantic gestures and remember to be delighted with each other's romantic ideas, thoughts and gifts and to show your appreciation.

Personal physical gestures are easy, free and the most endearing signs of love of all. Romantic touch gives the gentlest hint of sensuality alluding to your physical rapport, not ever pushing it. It's more about a special lightness between you – uplifting you and making you both glow with happiness. Hold that kind of love in your hand with any and every caress. Same with a look. Eyes meeting, let them send, and receive, your messages of love. Make other gestures, too, every day in all kinds of ways. No need to spend a lot – as ever it's the thought that's the true gift. A single flower can be devastatingly romantic, one chocolate carefully chosen for your partner because it's their very favourite can be worlds better than a box of the ones you prefer. It's about knowing each other really well. What will really please them and speak of your love? If you don't know, enjoy finding out. And always notice and show your pleasure in each other's gestures of romance.

MAKE TIME FOR ROMANCE

Giving some thought to and making time to be together is the heart of romance. Planning or taking advantage of opportunities that open up to spend time together as a couple is pure romance. There is no greater compliment than giving your time and full attention to each other. Again, it doesn't have to involve money. A walk through the park, for example, is a lovely expression of romance, as is any outing or activity that will feel good for both of you. Being in the car together is a great opportunity too – a special encapsulated time to enjoy each other's proximity and company. Now and then take a short break or longer holiday; again they are a great environment for romance. There's something about travelling together and resting or adventuring far from home that's stunningly romantic. Plan and enjoy. But remember that your home and your everyday life is where romance lives too. It's up to the two of you to notice it and love and nurture it. It will bless your lives, your relationship and your happiness. It's a gift that only a couple who love each other have and it's a great treasure.

Putting it all together

Don't let life jade you into thinking romance is in some way irrelevant or too frivolous now you're older. Actually it's always relevant because it's a breath of fresh air that keeps your love breathing steadily and strong. And nothing wrong with a little frivolity – this life can be pretty hard at times so take the chance romance offers to dance with the fun and tenderness of romance. Let it touch you with its simplicity and sweetness.

Love begins with romance and when romance continues to flourish, it helps love flourish too. No need, ever, to let it end. Love can last without it but, with it, it's even better – happier, shining brighter, and a more gorgeous and fun place to be.

And it's so easy – really just adopting a romantic attitude of mind. Opt for that attitude every day, orienting yourself to think warmly of your partner and how you can please them in any one of a myriad romantic ways.

Take care to appreciate any such gestures you receive from each other, especially if they are unaccustomed overtures into romance. Genuinely welcoming them is an equal part of the spirit of romance too. Like any compliment, it will shine if warmly and graciously received and as you reciprocate, you together light a beacon of love that lights up your togetherness now and for ever into the future.

Romance isn't a mystery, though it may feel mysteriously beautiful. It's love distilled purely and it gives a very special happiness that can feel almost intoxicating or simply give you a warm glow. And as a couple it's purely in your own hands to look after and enjoy. Treasure it and the happiness it gives you both.

46 Enjoy your own interests independently and share some too

> 'There is a you, lying dormant. A potential within you to be realized. There is more of you than you are presently aware of. Perhaps the only peace and joy in life lies in the pursuit of and the development of this potential.' Leo Buscaglia

> 'Don't give up your own opinions. Don't change your own beliefs. They were part of you before you were in the relationship and they should stay part of you.' Amanda Sposato

> 'It is not our purpose to become each other; it is to recognize each other, to learn to see the other and honour him for what he is.' Hermann Hesse

> 'How wrong is it for a woman to expect the man to build the world she wants, rather than to create it herself?' Anaïs Nin

> 'It's not a good idea to live in each other's pockets. Have your own lives.' Gwen Soane

Having your own individual interests is vital for your sense of personal identity and gives each of you and your relationship an extra dimension. One of the lovely things about a relationship is the way you merge your lives in many ways – it's comfortable, intimate and mutually supportive, but certain hobbies, studies and other interests are yours along with, of course, your thoughts and ideas. They enable your uniqueness – the essential person your partner fell in love with and vice versa. Veer too much towards each other's and you risk losing your soul and character – the very things that make you and your partner your selves.

It also adds a special vitality to your life to have your own ideas and activities and gives you a strong sense of self and therefore self-esteem that's very precious.

It's really helpful and affirming if you approve and encourage each other's need and right to do your own thing respectively. It shows you understand them and wish them personal fulfilment aside from the fulfilment you both find in your love and interaction.

It's also good to share some activities. The Secret of doing this happily is to genuinely take an interest and not feign it. So choose carefully what you'll both be able to thoroughly enjoy together. Faking it will become a burden and when you give up on it or show your boredom there'll be disappointment all round, so go for hobbies or other interests that really catch your imagination and excite you in some way.

Maintaining interests of your own gives a double dose of interest to your relationship – you've something fresh to talk about, something of your own outside your life together.

Sharing some interests is fun too and having the same pleasures and insights in them is a lovely feeling that draws you close. I love the Herman Hesse quote – that seeing each other following your respective paths gives insights into your characters and in recognition you see and honour each other.

Happiness in your relationship is not to merge into one being but to cherish your own and each other's uniqueness.

BE PASSIONATE ABOUT YOUR INDIVIDUAL INTERESTS

Keep your own interests vibrant, satisfying and constant and follow them persistently and passionately. They are part of who you are – the person your partner fell in love with. Same with them – their own interests are part of their character and their being. Be proactive in initiating and developing any new ones that appeal and cultivating and maintaining existing ones. It can be tempting, particularly early on in a relationship, to try to take over your partner's or have them opt into yours. While it's fine to share a few interests, resist any impulse to share all. Only agree to share something or follow an activity or pursuit together if you are both happy about it and if it genuinely appeals – never coerce each other. Do keep each other in the frame, though, by talking about what you've been doing. That way, neither of you will feel shut out or aggrieved at being left alone but will be happy you've enjoyed yourself. Interests, studies, sports, games keep our bodies and minds alert and they are enjoyable at the time but also, importantly, give you a pleasant feeling of satisfaction afterwards and this is a real tonic not just in your life generally but for your partner and your relationship too.

BE CLEAR ABOUT IT IF YOU WANT TO ENJOY AN INTEREST INDIVIDUALLY

There may be times when in your heart you know you want your interest to be yours alone but your partner tries to insist on joining you. When this is so, acknowledge your need or wish to keep it to yourself and stand firm. Explain to your partner it's your thing and that's how it's going to stay. Be very clear about it and stand firm. Honesty is the best policy. Once they understand it isn't that you don't want to follow the interest with them but that you want to do it alone because you feel it's fundamentally your thing is reasonable and, once they know this and consider it logically, completely understandable. So don't feel guilty about it. Your pleasure in your hobbies will encourage their joy for you and at the same time encourage them to develop their own interests too. It's good for you as a couple to keep some independence and to cherish your own and each other's individuality.

DECIDE WHICH INTERESTS YOU'D BOTH LIKE TO SHARE

Do some things together. Have a think about which ones you might both like. Listen to your heart – if there's an interested, uplifting feeling of anticipation it may be one you'll enjoy. If your heart sinks at the thought, ask yourself if your reluctance is due to a spurious fear you'd actually like to conquer, but if not and it's simply something you're not keen on doing, say no to it. Life is too short to spend chunks of it following someone else's enthusiasm that does nothing for you. Don't be persuaded against your will to attend anything that you know isn't and never will be for you. If you're open-minded it's different; by all means give it a go and then decide if you're going to take it up. Doing something that you both thoroughly enjoy is one of life's and your relationship's blessings. Remember – don't coerce each other into going along with an interest, don't pretend to like something doing something you don't. But if you think you could share your partner's passion for an interest and they'd like you to, or you're happy to share one of yours they're interested in, go for it and enjoy your togetherness to the full.

Putting it all together

Keeping some of your own interests to your respective selves signifies a healthy degree of independence and autonomy that contributes not just to the health of your relationship but your overall happiness together. You tacitly say 'I'm a woman/man with my own life, my own interests and passions. I'm also your partner, beloved of you and loving you deeply too. Sometimes we'll do things together and that will be great, and sometimes we'll go it alone with our own enthusiasms and that's fine too.' It's good to know and ensure that your love and your relationship isn't a controlling alliance and codependence that could engulf your individuality, but a complementary inter-dependence pleasurable in itself and in the independence and individuality you both value. Your unique personalities and minds are of course vital to each of you and give you your zest for life and love, and your relationship will be all the more so for appreciating this and, when you both wish, sharing some interests.

Always remember, and be prepared to reclaim when necessary your right and need to be your unique, special individual and independent selves and love that about each other. Your freedom of thought and interests is part of your intrinsic happiness and it enables a vigorous, delighted interest in each other's interests because you know they spell the real people you are.

Celebrate your own and each other's interests, your independence and your individual characters. Celebrate, too, the activities you enjoy alone and share.

They sing the song of your lives and your life together. They give great happiness and fulfilment that filters into your relationship, enriching it and feeling great.

47

Loving the world and lightening up about it

> *'Every spirit builds itself a house; and beyond its house a world; and beyond its world, a heaven.'* Ralph Waldo Emerson

> *'A sense of wonder reminds us of just how vast the unknown is and how much we have to learn each day.'* Beth Burns

> *'One cannot help but be in awe when one contemplates the mysteries of eternity, of life, of the marvellous structure of reality. It is enough if one tries merely to comprehend a little of this mystery every day. Never lose a holy curiosity.'* Albert Einstein

> *'When we plant the seeds of fascination and respect for other people, we are teaching tolerance and peace.'* Charlotte Davis Kasl

> *'No man or woman can be strong, gentle, pure and good, without the world being better for it and without someone being helped and comforted by the very existence of that goodness.'* Phillip Brooks

Many people go through life without seeing – really seeing – the world around them. This Secret which lights up a relationship as well as your individual life, is recognizing the beauty and wonder that's all around us, all the time. It's there for the noticing, and when you notice it, you resonate with the extraordinary mystery of life and can't help but feel uplifted and happy. That aura surrounds you and reflects on everyone around you and especially, of course, on your partner.

As in Secret 37, what a difference there is when your partner is positive, curious about and interested in life. It makes you interested, reminds you that there is wonder and joy out there, fills you with an excitement that may glow quietly or touch you with an invigorating excitement. Either way it's a tonic. Apathy, on the other hand, or a tired resignation that we are somehow failing our planet or it is failing us, is exhausting to live with and exhausting to be around.

Best of all is when the two of you join in appreciation of this amazing world we live in. It's there for the seeing, the experiencing, the enjoying, the fulfilment, the wonder. It's free, it's beautiful – it's truly a miracle.

A miracle? Absolutely. Whether you subscribe to a religious belief that the world came into being at the decision of a creator, or that it somehow started in another way – a chemical reaction for example (although that of course begs the question – how did the chemicals arrive in the first place?!) it is the most extraordinarily complex world that whether by chance or thought has evolved into a wonderland of beauty, symmetry and often pure perfection in the way the myriad life forms and systems thrive and interact.

This happiness is there for the choice and taking of any one of us.

You and your partner, every day, can feel the wonder, relish your curiosity about life, joy at the beauty, feel the goodness. It will light up your relationship. It's a rarely observed Secret of happiness in a relationship but it's a truly golden one. Use it and shine with awareness of the joy of our world and nature.

BEWARE A CYNICAL WORLD VIEW AND CHOOSE A POSITIVE, CONSTRUCTIVE ATTITUDE

Endless cynicism and pessimism about our future is depressing for both the cynic and their partner. Instead, get the worrying media reports about climate change, our destruction of the rainforests and other beautiful areas, etc., in perspective. Where you can, do something positive to help protect our planet, for example looking after your patch well and lobbying for more responsibility internationally. Refuse to be downhearted. The world has been through many changes and we can only do our best to help it survive the way we know it – sinking into apathy or depression won't help whereas your positivity may be useful in some way. Cheer each other up and on, reminding each other not to be apathetic or negative. Your relationship may be a tiny part of the whole kaleidoscope but it may have more impact than you realize and it's important for your own happiness, in any case, to make it a hopeful, positive place to be.

TAKE CONTROL OF YOUR OWN WORLD

You can't control the behaviour of others but you can look after your own. Be the best you that's possible. Be true and kind and good-hearted and positive. Be the kind of partner you would want to go out with. That way you'll look after your love of yourself, your partner's love for you and the contentment, peace and general feelgood factor of your interaction and life together. As you live positively this way, notice how your love-life attitude subtly – or sometimes dramatically maybe – affects others' behaviour. I find when I'm loving, courteous, kind and warm that's how others are around me. If on the other hand I'm grouchy and expectant of bad behaviour, surprise surprise, that's what I'll see. We are magnets for behaviour that reflects our expectations. How does this help your relationship? It's very simple: the more you practise being a lovely person who it's lovely to be with, the happier your relationship will be. We're all part of this world. Feel how good humanity is and relish your part in it.

TAKE DELIGHT IN YOUR PART IN THIS LIFE

Understand – and feel your understanding deeply and joyously – that you are a part of the life of the world. Two beings who are here for your lifespan and out of all the billions of people on Earth have chosen to be together and to love each other. That's pretty amazing isn't it? We don't understand the whole science of it. We don't understand the spirituality we often sense if we take the time to feel it. But science and spirituality are both there, a part of each other, part of the whole as you are. If the two of you share your wonder and curiosity and sense of awe at all this, it creates a very special bond between you that seems to resonate in tune. It's a rare thing for someone to appreciate the world and our chance to be here, and even rarer for a couple to share the joy in it all. But I hope you do for it's a very special Secret that will give an extra dimension of happiness to your relationship and your love. Share the wonder.

Putting it all together

As I started writing this section I first wrote of the danger of apathy and resignation in a relationship along with a general blindness to the beauty of love and life. As I wrote that way, I felt narky and discomfited. If I'd been with someone I'd have given off, I'm sure, a distinctly negative vibe that would have affected them adversely too. So I started afresh with the positives that we get when, instead, we see, appreciate and, especially, share the wonder of our world. Immediately it was as though I made a wonderful emotional leap – springing into my usual happiness that anyone around me, again, would have shared.

I tell you about this because it highlights how important it is to look positively and in celebration at our gift of life here in this extraordinarily beautiful, complex world. We are a minute part of it – just think – there are countless other universes beyond ours – and yet here we are, living, feeling, loving and with the gift of thought and willpower so that we can choose to appreciate our lives, the love we share, the astonishing beauty of our world and hugely importantly, our wonder at it all.

It's especially fantastic if you both sense this gift we have of life and share your gladness, thankfulness and joy in it. When you were first in love you probably felt it very strongly and resonated with the excitement of life and love. You always can. It hasn't gone away. It's always there.

Sharing the sense of mystery and beauty is a powerful, wonderful aspect of love and brings a unique kind of happiness in a relationship. Feel it, live it, love it. And let it light up your love for each other.

48 Creating a home you both love

66 *'Home is where the heart is.'* Pliny the Elder

66 *'Make your home into a place you're glad to come home to. Make it so it sings to your hearts.'* Penny Berridge

66 *'Where thou art, that is home.'* Emily Dickinson

66 *'The home should be the treasure chest of living.'* Le Corbusier

66 *'Home interprets heaven. Home is heaven for beginners.'* Charles Henry Parkhurst

Our homes are fundamental to our happiness. They're where we rest, play, sometimes work and generally where we spend a large amount of time. They are where we live and where we love – the backdrop for your togetherness. So it's vital for both of you and the way you get on to be happy in the home you share.

Fortunately, this Secret of love and life doesn't mean having loads of money. You can have a home you love however humble or grand it is. Three of the basic needs for happiness are a roof over our heads, warmth and love. Given the first two, with the right attitude you and your partner can build a haven where your love can flourish.

Attitude is everything. What to one person might seem small and lowly might to another be sheer luxury. Any home, with love and the right attitude, can be a piece of heaven. So this Secret is all about recognizing the potential of your home, if you don't already, realizing the joy and contentment it has to offer you and together lovingly looking after it.

Ah – but you may have such different tastes and thoughts about the nature of 'home'? That's fine. No matter how diverse your opinions you can find compromise or work out the best way to resolve them so that home is still an oasis of comfort and pleasure for you both. Couples do this in all kinds of ways – we're all different and as with all the Secrets if you wish to make it work for you it will.

Coming home to each other is a refuge from the outside world, a place where you can totally relax, be yourselves, and simply enjoy each other's proximity and company. Filled with your love the atmosphere is replenishing and uplifting, soothing and healing. It's a safe place to 'hold' you as you live through the experiences and resultant emotions of the years. It's home – the dwelling place of your bodies, your spirit and the love you share.

Your home is your sanctuary, your partner's and your relationship's – and it's yours, blissfully, to create.

MAKE YOUR HOME A HAVEN OF PEACE

Agree to keep it as an oasis of peace and replenishment and don't allow it, ever, to turn into a vicious battleground. Think of it not just as somewhere comfortable to be but a place that hugs you, keeps you safe and protects you from strife. Decide and pledge that any disputes you have will be constructively, amicably resolved. No shouting, no door slamming. In fact ban all violence – and that includes nastiness and insults. Noise and abuse of any other kind sabotage the pleasant atmosphere of your surroundings. And homes definitely do have an atmosphere and, I think, a personality.

I remember once someone telling me about their unhappy relationship. Unable in the moment to see any hope of reconciliation or resolution they flew into a rage and left, slamming the front door so hard the whole house shook and seemed to weep both for the disturbance to its peace and for the sadness of her anger. Refuse to let hostility between you infect your home. Sort out issues positively as and when they come up and remember, even when you have differences, as you inevitably will – that you love each other. It may sound simplistic – but simplicity in this context works. Instantaneously, the minute you bring to mind the love you fundamentally share despite your current scrap, you feel better. Then you're – immediately again – in a better place to decide on the best solution to the problem for both of you. This way your home holds you and your resolution safely, allowing positive repair and healing. Peaceful, your home will always be a happy place to be. Cherish it as a peaceful zone and it will hug the two of you close.

A COMFORTABLE AND SENSUALLY APPEALING HOME IS A TEAM EFFORT

As a team, enjoy making or keeping your home a place of comfort that looks good, appeals to all your senses and makes you feel good. How you share this will be your own unique arrangement. Agree who's going to do what – you may be glad to shoulder certain aspects individually or take turns – it's up to every couple to decide what's best for their preferences and tastes. Some couples decide that one or other of them will look after the interior design – the choice of colour schemes, furniture, soft furnishings, artwork and other decorations, etc., while the other looks after the technical and/ or practical side of things. Others like to choose it all together. Or you might decide to take it in turns to make decisions, or allocate one room for one of you to look after, another for the other to take care of. It doesn't matter if you have differing taste and, if so, be careful not to criticize each other's ideas – it's very personal and can hurt! With a willingness to respect each other's preferences and either reach compromise or take turns at having your choice, you can still have a great deal of fun and satisfaction in making your home a gorgeous environment you both love.

SORT OUT WHO IS GOING TO DO WHAT AND ENJOY IT

Reach agreement in day-to-day household chores and the minutiae of running a home. As ever, follow the golden trio: talk, compromise, respect. Just about everything to do with your home is a joint responsibility – make it a pleasure – it can be a huge one! Flexibility and willingness are the keys to taking on and delegating the various things that need doing. It's amazing, too, how getting on with it all with a cheerful attitude instantly takes the hard-work, dreary element of it away. Doing things with love in your hearts pulls you close too. It's fun to 'make house' – something all kids dream of doing some day and here you are, grown-ups with total freedom to make your home exactly how you want it to be. Fulfil tasks with love in your hearts and feel the closeness, energy and satisfaction it gives you to the full. Value your home-making as a big part of your relationship – it is crucial to your happiness and a delightful aspect of it and by taking loving care of your home you'll care for your relationship lovingly too.

Putting it all together

Home will be the biggest backdrop to your relationship as the years go by and it's where, lovingly looked after and shared equally between you in all its various aspects, your relationship will flourish, held safe by its comfort and brightened by its visual appeal. Your home, whatever its size, can be your palace and your heaven on earth. Make it a place of love and peace, a place to rest and heal, to enjoy life as you wish to feel, quite simply, at home.

It's very, very precious to feel at home. So taking care to make it appeal to your senses is immensely satisfying. The look of your home, the sounds, the feelgood factor and atmosphere the two of you create are a huge part in the way you feel about life generally. Your home is a part of you, an expression of your tastes and ideas, a sign that you like comfort and deserve it. Of course you do – as individuals and as a couple you are free to make the kind of home you both like and when you do, it hugs you.

Having a home you both love that reflects your personalities signals not just your love of life but your love for each other.

Peace, shelter, comfort, love. Your home is at the heart of your happiness together. As Penny Berridge said: 'Make your home into a place you're glad to come home to. Make it so it sings to your hearts.'

Enjoy it – and your relationship will sing with the happiness too.

49 Surviving families and friends

❝ *'A happy family is but an earlier heaven.'* George Bernard Shaw

❝ *'The greatest thing in family life is to take a hint when a hint is intended-and not to take a hint when a hint isn't intended.'* Robert Frost

❝ *'Very small practical changes can continue to multiply into greatly increased happiness.'* Robin Skynner

❝ *'Admitting something's wrong is the first step to putting it right.'* Rosie Hallett

❝ *'Language affects behaviour. There are those who have created a positive linguistic environment. Their words are joyful, pleasant, reflective of the beautiful, reinforcing of the good.'* Leo Buscaglia

Families! As a couple you have your own respective sets of relatives and friends and, as well as the in-laws you gained when you got together, perhaps there are also 'outlaws' as a friend likes to call her 'second family' of ex-partners and ex-in-laws and her stepchildren and grandchildren. And then there's the family, if you become parents, that you create. All in all, you probably share quite a network of family interactions between people with different loyalties, some powerfully strong, and perhaps many prejudices. It's seen by some as a minefield of emotions! But with love in your hearts and a willingness to accept and adapt to each other, your shared family can be wonderful and hugely rewarding for you as a couple.

The knack is to realize and enjoy the wealth of opportunities for love, support and fun as well as a treasure trove of wonderfully accessible wisdom and experience. Like all the secrets of happiness, it starts with a positive decision, a flexible attitude and bucket-loads of tolerance and kindness.

But what about when your family or your partner's is unhealthy in some way – what then? How can you remain positive about people who seem unhinged or determined to dislike you and/or your partner? Holding on to the possibility that, at least one day if not now, things can get better is the key, along with the firm resolve that in the meantime you'll remain a team as a couple, undivided by others' negative emotions.

Also, knowing that you have each other's love and approval whatever is going on in the family, strengthens your relationship and lets happiness thrive regardless of any hostile factions.

Quite often all it takes to bring about change is making the decision to get on with the families as best you can, no matter what, with a willingness to be friends at any stage, even if now they won't enable that. Love is strong and with an ample supply of it along with willingness to make practical, positive adjustments, the happiness of you and your partner can survive and even thrive within the family dynamics.

KEEP YOUR NEGATIVE OPINIONS OF YOUR IN-LAWS TO YOURSELF

One of the best ways of keeping good relationships with your and your partner's relatives, and surviving and resolving any disputes and hostility, is to remember the art of keeping your negative opinions to yourself. Banging on about your mother-in-law's faults, for instance, will do nothing to endear you to your partner and would probably only succeed in making them unhappy or defensive. Silence is golden is a great maxim when it comes to your respective opinions about each other's in-laws. It's just not fair to try to divide each other's loyalties. But that doesn't mean pretending nothing's wrong. Ignored, problems live on and may escalate. Faced and well-handled, the positive adjustments you make can open the way for harmony and friendship. Don't let your partner abuse your relatives either. In either case, instead of reacting in a hostile manner to them – even if they seem to be hostile to you – think how you can turn it around and open the way to get on well together or at least maintain a comfortable truce.

OUST FEELINGS OF JEALOUSY

Don't let jealousy come between you and your relatives or in-laws. We all feel jealous or envious sometimes – it's human nature, so don't feel ashamed but do act positively to oust it. The best way is often to say to yourself: 'Hey – where is this feeling coming from – why am I so jealous?' Just acknowledging it and facing the reason is often all it takes for it to disappear. If it persists or recurs, reflect that we're all different and will sometimes be more or less successful than others and have more or less than them one way or another. Thankfully, we're all free to be different and do our own thing and thank goodness for that. Whatever happens to you in life, you are a unique person and have an individual spirit and character. Be the best you can be and do your best in life and don't waste any time or energy on wishing you were someone else. Above all, don't resent each other's love for your respective families. It's a different kind of love to couple love and the loves can co-exist happily and complement each other. Be glad your partner loves their family and vice versa and realize that it's not a threat to the love the two of you share.

ACCEPT THAT YOU'RE ALL DIFFERENT

All families and groups of friends are different, so accept gracefully the differences between your respective sets of loved ones. Instead of bemoaning them, be glad for them – after all your partner wouldn't be the person he or she is if it weren't for their family background and friends. Often, acceptance is simply a matter of shrugging negative feelings and prejudices off your shoulders and thinking: 'They are as they are – let's focus on finding things to like about them and letting that, with a loving attitude, maybe even become love one day.' Once you decide to be not only tolerant but to look for the good in them, see how much easier it is to make a fuss of them and generally be nicer to and with them. Notice how your interaction improves and enjoy the new positivity. It's virtually always reciprocated – one of the wonderful miracles of life. So think of little ways you can light up their lives – and see how it reflects beautifully in your relationship with your partner too. For life is so much easier if you not only tolerate but make an effort to like each other's relatives and friends. It makes you feel more loving towards each other too and, all in all, adds to the happiness you share together.

Putting it all together

We can't escape our families – unless of course we completely cut ourselves off from them – and then we'd miss such an opportunity. For all family networks offer a tremendous opportunity to enrich your relationship with your partner. Even simply embracing your solidarity as a couple can give you a feeling of strength and security. But how much better if you can get on with each other's relatives and the further extended families you share and embrace the chances for loving contact and friendships, for warmth, support and camaraderie – for a feeling not just of being a team as a couple but a team within a larger, multi-stranded wonderful team where all the members are rooting for each other.

Of course, families aren't always harmonious. Irritations, jealousies, suspicions, etc. are pretty much certain to occur at times with so many individuals and backgrounds coming together. The Secret is to notice them and pay positive attention without instantly going into aggressive and/or defensive modes. That way you can think logically how you or they or, probably, all of you can best make adjustments that will improve the situation, heal rifts and enable good communication to continue so that you can always live diplomatically and negotiate settlements that please you all and promote new or renewed harmony.

Love, as ever, is a vital key. If you can't find it in your heart to love your relatives or in-laws at the moment, your love as a couple for each other will hold you safe in the familial discord and remind you to behave kindly and positively because that's the kind of people you are, and because you love each other and know that family is important.

Respect and care for each other's feelings this way and acceptance and tolerance and a way of finding things to like about them will become your natural way of being around your own and each other's families.

Above all, love each other, and you and your families may well do the same.

Let the light of love shine throughout with your loving attitude and bask in the light of happiness as it reflects in your relationship.

50 Looking out for each other's wellbeing

'If every man would make his prime concern the comfort and wellbeing of his wife and every wife make her chief concern the comfort and wellbeing of her husband, we would have very little divorce in the land.' Gordon B. Hinckley

'Indifference and neglect often do much more damage than outright dislike.' J. K. Rowling

'Too often we underestimate the power of a touch, a smile, a kind word, a listening ear, an honest compliment or the smallest act of caring, all of which have the potential to turn a life around.' Leo Buscaglia

'The purpose of a relationship is not to have another who might complete you, but to have another with whom you might share your completeness.' Neale Donald Walsch

'When you're in a relationship and it's good, even if nothing else in your life is right, you feel like your whole world is complete.' Keith Sweat

Wellbeing! A sense that, whatever else is going on in our lives, all is somehow well with us and within us. It may also be a feeling of the essential goodness of life and love. It's the understanding and sense of the homeostasis we enjoy as living creatures – a continuous healing and repair of our bodies, minds and souls and your relationship too. A sense, above all, that you are loved and that you love.

Love is something we can all feel – it's there for you now and always. It exists inside you and already or potentially in your relationship. It's there for the noticing. So often a couple doesn't feel it because they're so busy with all the minutiae of life as well as the big issues, with roving thoughts and worries that they succumb to negativity: 'I haven't got time for xxx', 'I haven't got the energy…', 'I can't, I can't, I can't'. Or we get irritated by and critical of our nearest and dearest for no particular reason, except it just happens. And then we're too apathetic or busy with other things to realize that, actually, of course we love them and would miss them to bits if they weren't around anymore.

I want you, instead – more than all the other Secrets because it encompasses them all and makes it easy for you to remember them and live them – to pause often and feel your wellbeing and look after it. If it seems to be missing, call it back into your life. Call it into your being, your world and give it your full attention. It's up to you and it's up to your partner. Together you can call it into your relationship. And as you invite it in and welcome it with every cell of your body and mind, the feeling will be there for you.

It's all about a sense of peace and that you are in the right place this day and with the right person. If you are in good physical and mental health you register that particular kind of wellbeing and feel your whole body and your brain and spirit rejoicing. It's a kind of hum – a resonance, a recognition, a giving of thanks for the life you have and the love you share.

LOOK AFTER YOUR HEALTH

Care for your own health – it's the first step in looking after your wellbeing. We have these amazingly complicated bodies that despite their complexity generally work brilliantly well. Have great respect for all the different systems and do all you can to take care of them brilliantly. Follow the general guidelines of eating a good, balanced diet to keep your digestion as healthy as possible and to nourish your whole body and mind. Exercise to keep your muscles fit and your circulation good. Go easy on the things that aren't good for you in excess, choosing to see them as occasional treats – you'll enjoy them all the more. Take a keen interest in food values and the way you can promote good health in all kinds of ways.

Once you get used to the idea of looking after your health and giving your natural healing strategies and functions the best chance of working well, it becomes second nature and it feels really good. Look after your mind too. Think deeply and widely to keep your brain functioning well and keep it lively and alert by taking a keen interest in all kinds of things and by continuing to learn as much as you can. My dad used to say: 'Your brain is your most precious asset. Look after it and learn something new every day.' All these years on, I still try to do this and it always makes me happy when I do and find myself thinking: 'That's interesting – I must remember that!' It feels good and when you and your partner find life fascinating and fulfilling it gives your relationship a huge sense of wellbeing too.

LOOK OUT FOR EACH OTHER'S HEALTH

Care for each other's health. You're hugely fortunate to be in a relationship – not only are our chances of experiencing a feeling of wellbeing enhanced if we are in loving relationships, but you can also help your partner look after their health and vice versa. Delicious and nutritious meals are not only good for your bodies but the planning and cooking are fun when it's for the two of you and enjoying eating them together is great too as we saw in Secret 18. It's also much easier to maintain weights that are right for you if you eat together and both keep an eye on the calories and carbohydrates. Exercising together – going for long walks, for example, or going swimming – encourages you to keep it up on a regular basis. Remind each other, urge each other on and enjoy the feeling of complicity and camaraderie. Do all you can to maximize your own and each other's health and compliment each other on your fitness. And get into the habit of noticing and being appreciative of the wellbeing you both enjoy. This is a vital element of happiness between the two of you as it's so mutually satisfying and encourages a feeling of positivity that permeates your whole relationship. It also makes you remember how much you cherish each other and feel cherished. It's one of the very nicest caring aspects of a relationship and so easy to keep fresh and vibrant.

MAKE FEELING YOUR WELLBEING A HABIT

Get the wellbeing habit. Just as we can choose whether to take a positive or negative attitude, so you can choose to sense a feeling of wellbeing. Pause now and then, even in the busiest of most stressful of days, to relax and feel a deep sense of peace within you. Say to yourself: 'All is well' (or, if you are in a difficult or sad time: 'All will be well again, one day, and meanwhile I will feel the memory of wellbeing to see me through this time.') Be supportive of your partner and receive their support well too. Encourage with every part of your being each other's wellbeing.

Sadly, our bodies may be subject to illness but the habit of maintaining the sense of wellbeing is a huge help in coping well with symptoms and can even speed and assist the healing process. Empathy and love are tremendously soothing and helpful, too, of course, in enduring illness and they are an intrinsic part of wellbeing as well as feeling good in themselves. Our bodies and minds want us to cope, to get well or to feel as well as possible in any circumstances. Recognize the gift you have of shared love and togetherness. Feel how good it is, mind, body and soul. Be alert to the presence of wellbeing in your lives and in your life together and feel the wellbeing. It is your great gift. Feel the goodness of it and give thanks.

Putting it all together

None of us knows for sure what will happen tomorrow let alone in the years ahead. But you do know this moment, this space when time stands still as you register your being right now. How important then – how vital and crucial and downright essential – that you appreciate your gift of life and celebrate the miracle. Be aware of love, too – the love between you and your partner and the love in other parts of your life. And be aware of the love all around you, too, for the world is full of love – it's there in every nanoparticle of the miracle of creation and in the way people generally get on very well together as well as in our special relationships.

Focus on feeling the buzz, the resonance of life in your being and in your relationship.

Register your wellbeing every day. If at this time things are hard or sad for you my heart goes out to you. Know that change is possible and hold tightly to the knowledge that your sense of wellbeing can return. Your natural homeostasis – your body and mind's constant rebalancing, healing process – is always working. Help it along with your faith in it, your courage and your love.

When you recognize your ability to experience and always return to a sense of wellbeing, your whole life will be uplifted. Your happiness will pass naturally to your partner and when the two of you sense each other's health and healing and general all-round wellbeing, your relationship will benefit too.

Look after your selves and look after each other and feel the intrinsic sense of wellbeing.

I wish you love and happiness. With all my heart I wish you well.